DEANS and DEVELOPMENT

Making the Case for Supporting the Liberal Arts and Sciences

Council of Colleges of Arts & Sciences

DEANS and DEVELOPMENT:
Making the Case for Supporting the Liberal Arts and Sciences
Edited by Anne-Marie McCartan and Carl J. Strikwerda
ISBN 978-0-615-96691-5

Printed in the United States of America

The Council of Colleges of Arts & Sciences (CCAS) was founded in 1965 to provide opportunities for deans of arts and sciences to discuss issues of common concern and to advocate for the intellectual stature and the public understanding of the disciplines of the arts and sciences. Today, CCAS represents over 700 deans of arts and sciences and 1000 associate and assistant deans. The Executive Office resides at The College of William & Mary, hosted by the Dean of the Faculty of Arts and Sciences.

PO Box 8795
Williamsburg VA 23187-8795 USA
www.ccas.net

To purchase this book, write ccas@wm.edu

Cover design by Jean Pokorny

TO OUR FACULTY MEMBERS IN ARTS AND SCIENCES
whose good work allows us to make the case for the liberal arts

Table of Contents

reef fishes, Danilowicz has carried out research at locations ranging from Iceland to French Polynesia. To support his research along with student success initiatives, he has been principle investigator or co-PI on externally funded grants totaling over $11 million. Danilowicz has attended CCAS meetings annually since 2005, and presently serves as the chair of the committee on research universities. Development is a continual learning process; he is enjoying daily lessons along with the A&S development team of Lauren Kidd, Craig Jackson, Mauralee Boersma, and Melissa Smith. Go team!

Richard Finkelstein

Richard Finkelstein is Dean of the College of Arts and Sciences at the University of Mary Washington in Fredericksburg, Virginia. He received his B.A. from Williams College and his Ph.D. from the University of Chicago. Prior to his work at Mary Washington, he was Chair of the English Department at SUNY Geneseo, where he taught for many years, and a faculty member at Northeastern University. He has led or served as an officer on not-for-profit boards of organizations that address the needs of young children. He is spearheading an initiative in Fredericksburg to build a Climate and Environmental Action Plan for the University and the region. His academic research and writing focuses on Shakespeare and Renaissance Drama.

Pamela S. Gates

Pamela Gates is Professor of English and Dean of the College of Humanities and Social and Behavioral Sciences at Central Michigan University. She received her Ph.D. from Michigan State University and has been at CMU since 1987. Her academic teaching and research is on literature for children and young adults with a focus on multicultural literature; she currently co-hosts a book review radio show for the WCMU PBS station. She has attended CCAS meetings since she began her work in the Dean's office in 2001—first as associate Dean and now as Dean for five years. She has been fortunate to work have worked with two outstanding development officers during her time in the dean's office—Alison Miller and Lesa Smith. Their professional knowledge and their commitment to the programs in the college has generated millions of dollars in gifts over the past seven years to support the students and faculty and it is a privilege to have worked with them both.

Julie Candler Hayes

Julie Candler Hayes is Professor of French and Dean of the College of Humanities and Fine Arts at the University of Massachusetts Amherst. She previously served as a department chair both at UMass and the University of Richmond. A scholar of the French Enlightenment, she also writes on contemporary literary theory, the history and theory of translation, and professional and institutional issues. The recipient of fellowships from the National Endowment for the Humanities and the National Humanities Center, she was honored by being named Chevalier in the Ordre des Palmes Académiques by the French government in 2010. In 2012-13, she served as president of the American Society for Eighteenth-Century Studies, an interdisciplinary scholarly organization. She is grateful to Lucia Miller, the Director of Development for the College of Humanities and Fine Arts, for her impeccable people skills and insights.

Anne-Marie McCartan

Since 2006, Anne-Marie has served as Executive Director of the Council of Colleges of Arts & Sciences. Previously she served as President of the Northwest Campus of Pima Community College (Tucson) and Provost and Dean of Faculty at Richard Bland College of the College of William & Mary (Petersburg, Virginia). She held other leadership positions with the Virginia Community College System, Rappahannock Community College, and the State Council of Higher Education for Virginia. She received her undergraduate degree (history) and master's degree (public administration) from the University of Washington and holds a doctorate of education from Harvard University. She is grateful to have had such a dedicated group of colleagues with whom to work in producing this volume.

Matthew C. Moen

Matthew C. Moen is Dean of the College of Arts and Sciences, Professor of Political Science, and Lohre Distinguished Professor at the University of South Dakota. Before returning to his native state in 2002, Dr. Moen worked for sixteen years at the University of Maine as a faculty member, department chair, and special assistant to the president. He published five books and was named University of Maine Trustee Professor. Past leadership roles include president of the New England Political Science Association, chairperson of the Professional Ethics Committee of the American Political Science Association, and president of the Council of Colleges of Arts and Sciences—the national arts and sciences dean's organization. He received a Ph.D. through the Carl Albert Congressional Studies Center at the University of Oklahoma, serving as a Congressional Fellow in the 1980s. He received a B.A. with honors from Augustana College, which honored him with its Alumni Achievement Award in 2005. Dr. Moen is part of a collaboration on interdisciplinarity in the academy that will be published by Oxford University Press, and he speaks and writes about the place of the liberal arts and sciences in the academy.

Carl J. Strikwerda

Carl J. Strikwerda is President and Professor of History at Elizabethtown College, in Elizabethtown, Pennsylvania. A graduate of Calvin College, he received his Ph.D. from the University of Michigan. As an Associate Dean in the College of Liberal Arts and Sciences at the University of Kansas and Dean of the Faculty of Arts and Sciences at the College of William and Mary, he was active in the Council of Colleges of Arts and Sciences and served as the Treasurer and a member of the Board of Directors of CCAS. He has enjoyed working with numerous donors and foundations to build academic and outreach programs. His academic interests are in the history of globalization, including teaching a course at Elizabethtown College on "Peace and War in a Global World." He would like to thank the following development officers, former deans, deans, and staff members with whom he has had the privilege to work over the last 15 years: Andrew Barry, David

Beidleman, Annie C. Davis, Geoffrey Feiss, Lesley Finney, Rich Kaler, Mark Kiselica, the late Terry Knoll Johnson, Linda Luvaas, Sally Mason, Sean Pieri, Barbara Salins, Bernadette Schroch, Joel Schwartz, Marty Thomas-Brume, William Tsutsui, and Kim Wilcox. You have been very patient. You have been good teachers.

D.J. Trela

D.J. Trela recently completed fourteen years as Dean of the College of Arts and Sciences at the University of Michigan—Flint. Prior to this appointment he served for nearly six years as Director of the School of Liberal Studies, and three as Chair of the Department of English, at Roosevelt University in Chicago. Trela, currently Professor of English, serves on the Board of the Flint Institute of Arts, and as Board Chair of the Flint Cultural Center Corporation. His background in fundraising includes serving on the Steering Committee for the UM-Flint Capital Campaign (2004–09), chairing the Development Task Force for the 2011–16 UM-Flint Strategic Plan, serving on the Development Committee of the FCCC, and many years of meeting with and cultivating donors. Particular thanks are due to his former Major Gift Officer, Ms. Shelly Hoffman, who taught him most of what he knows about the practical side of fundraising in a University environment.

Acknowledgements

It was a pleasure working with a group of deans who were willing to find time in their always-hectic schedules to reflect upon their experiences with development. It was not hard to motivate them to participate in this project as these deans have found that raising funds to support their college's priorities and programs is one of the more satisfying aspects of their jobs. During the course of preparing this volume, the CCAS Board of Directors has been unstinting in its support under the leadership of Mary Anne Fitzpatrick (University of South Carolina, CCAS President 2012-2013) and Nancy A. Gutierrez (University of North Carolina at Charlotte, CCAS President 2013-2014). As even good writers need professional checks, we thank John H. (Jay) Whaley, Jr., for copyediting the work, and Nicole Huff, our proofreader. Finally, CCAS is supported by a talented graphic designer, Jean Pokorny, who worked through the details of bringing the first book published by CCAS to fruition.

Whether made clear as an expectation by your president or provost, or initiated within Arts and Sciences itself, doing development—that is, creating the relationships that lead to successful fundraising—has become an increasingly important role for deans. Successful development experience also has become critical for those who wish to advance beyond the deanship.

Yet Arts and Sciences deans face unique challenges in fundraising. Professional-school deans can make a case for their special niche, and they often focus almost exclusively on graduate or professional education. The Arts and Sciences dean has to represent the crucial importance of the liberal arts—and often of undergraduate education as well—to prospective donors whose commitment to the life of the mind and learning for its own sake may be limited at best. Unlike their counterparts in professional schools, Arts and Sciences deans oversee a myriad of departments and interdisciplinary programs and intersect with every other office on campus. Most graduates who majored in the Arts and Sciences identify with the larger university or with their individual department, not with the Arts and Sciences college as a whole. Indeed, many may not even know that they received their education from a college of Arts and Sciences. Thus, they may consider giving donations either to the University or, perhaps, to their department, but rarely to the college of Arts and Sciences. In addition, University-based development offices wary of the politics of departmentally based faculties, the near-tribal hostilities between humanists and scientists, and squabbling departments within Arts and Sciences, are tempted to concentrate on professional school fundraising and avoid Arts and Sciences' needs.

Despite these challenges, private fundraising can yield great rewards to Arts and Sciences colleges, allowing them to educate their students in exciting new ways, strengthen faculty teaching and research, and make Arts and Sciences a more important part of the university. For those donors who truly wish to leave a legacy, and to help young people have the opportunities they deserve, private giving to Arts and Sciences holds the potential to have a significant impact on the next generation.

With this as context, the CCAS Board of Directors authorized its Executive Director to identify CCAS deans and former deans to prepare a book that would speak to the fundraising environment for Arts and Sciences deans. The authors of this volume have over 50 years of combined experience as deans. And, as is always the case with CCAS programs and services, who better than decanal peers to provide guidance, mentoring, ideas, and validation?

This book addresses these questions:

1. Why do people give money for "development," and what does a dean need to know about the complex world of University development to help his or her own college?
2. As only one player in this complex world, how can an Arts and Sciences dean best position the college to take advantage of the University offices that support development efforts?
3. Once you understand how you fit within your University's development world, how do you organize your office, staff, faculty, advisory boards, and other players to pull together to raise money for your college?
4. Now that you have all the organizational pieces in place, how do you go about finding and cultivating potential donors and knowing what and how much to ask for—in the long and short terms?
5. Given the particular fundraising challenges for deans of Arts and Sciences, how can you ensure that your college's priorities, programs, and initiatives receive top billing and that all (both within your college and the University) appreciate the potential to make the case for funding the liberal arts?

In Chapter 1 *(What is "Development," and What is the Role of the Arts and Sciences Dean?)* Carl Strikwerda provides an overview of fundraising terminology and principles. He begins by explaining why people give money to higher education, and how you as dean can position yourself to have your college priorities and programs brought to the attention of potential donors. For those not familiar with the full array of operations in a large University development office, he describes each of those offices and how a dean might best interact with them. The steps in approaching potential donors are covered, along with what needs to happen once the commitment of the donor is clear. Importantly, he offers cautionary tales for activities and efforts that might best be avoided.

Chapter 2 *(Arts and Sciences on Campus)*, by Matthew C. Moen, reminds the reader that the liberal arts are the historical and intellectual centerpiece of the American university. It outlines the particular challenges faced by Arts and Sciences deans, and shows how developing good relationships with the University's development staff and other university entities can work to your advantage.

The authors of Chapter 3 *(Organizing the Dean's Office for Development)*, Bret S. Danilowicz and Julie Chandler Hayes, explain how development is teamwork, and they provide a deeper explication of the roles that must be played in order to support your college's development strategy. They address an issue of interest to many deans: how external advisory boards can be used to further your development efforts.

D.J. Trela, along with Richard Finkelstein and Lori Vermeulen, provide the nuts-and-bolts details about raising funds in Chapter 4 *(Finding Money and Raising Funds)*. Fundraising is a science and an art, requiring a systematic approach to the endeavor while staying flexible and creative in identifying those who may be interested in the work of your college and explaining how, through cultivation and stewardship; they can become willing to contribute.

Finally, in Chapter 5 *(Making the Case for Arts and Sciences)*, David Boocker and Pamela S. Gates urge deans to be prepared to articulate a strong case for the value of the liberal arts. Further, they describe how you, as the liberal arts dean, can position yourself with funders to sell the importance of what is happening within your college. Both have had success by focusing on "messaging"—by having a clear message about their college to convey within the University and to potential donors, and by listening carefully to messages *from* potential donors about what they are passionate about and may be willing to support within Arts and Sciences.

Invariably there is some overlap in content among the chapters, but this has the advantage of allowing the reader to more readily appreciate the variety of approaches to development. The authors share examples and stories from their experience—be they victories or learning opportunities. All believe in the importance of fundraising and speak to the sense of fulfilment that can come from raising money for your college. One cannot read this volume without becoming convinced that development is not a scary, must-do-it function of a modern-day Arts and Science dean, but an achievable and satisfying endeavor. May you, too, find it to be so.

—Anne-Marie McCartan & Carl J. Strikwerda, Co-Editors

NOTES ON TERMINOLOGY:

University offices that raise private funds have different names. "Development" is the most common one, but "Advancement" is also used. An older term, "Endowment Association," is still encountered. At some institutions, "Advancement" refers to a group of offices that report to a vice president that includes development, communications, and alumni relations. At many public Colleges or Universities, non-profit foundations have been created to handle private funds more flexibly than is allowed by state government rules. These foundations are effectively the development arm of the College or University. At these public institutions "the Foundation" is a synonym for the development office, a reference that can be confusing to those in private higher education. To clarify matters in this volume, we will use "Development Office" as the generic term for the office at a College or University that raises private funds.

We use the term "dean of Arts and Sciences" in the broadest sense; that is, any dean with oversight for the disciplines encompassed by the liberal arts—whether they be housed in a single "college of Arts and Sciences," or segmented into units (Sciences, Humanities & Social Sciences, Letters & Sciences, and so forth) defined as assigned to a dean.

When referring to institutions, the terms University and College are used. A lowercase "c" is used for colleges of Arts and/or Sciences, and the term "college" is shorthand for a college or a school. "Department chairs" is synonymous with "department head."

1

What is "Development" and What is the Role of the Arts and Sciences Dean?

Carl J. Strikwerda

With money from additional tuition and government sources increasingly scarce, deans of Arts and Sciences must develop a robust development operation and build the supporting functions that make it successful. This chapter provides a basic introduction to fundraising and to the operations that support fundraising for an Arts and Sciences college. The primary focus will be on Arts and Sciences colleges that are within a larger University with multiple colleges or schools. Much of the material, however, also will be useful for an Arts and Sciences dean at a college without any professional schools, and where he or she is the only dean.

The best place to begin is to understand fundraising at the conceptual level and then move through the practical steps of raising funds. The first rule of being a good fundraiser, however, is to make a gift yourself. While it does not need to be a large gift, it is important to always lead by example. By making a gift, your donors will intuitively understand you to be saying "I believe, I support, and I hope that you'll join with me."

Understanding Development

Why should anyone give a substantial sum of money to a College or University? People give for many reasons, but the most important reasons are because they care about an institution in whose mission they believe, they want to pay someone back for the opportunities they were given, they want to support an activity at the institution such as the arts or women's issues that they are involved with in another part of their

Establishing clear priorities is hard work, but critical to the success of the development effort.

Once the college has forged a document setting its goals in priority order, the next step is to review it with a development officer who knows your institution's donor pool and can advise on your priorities. Some will be of little or no interest to your typical donor; any may need to be re-crafted and recast to attract interest. Others may not fit comfortably with development goals being pursued at the University level.

As described more fully in the chapter by Boocker and Gates, once your development goals are firmly established, it is time to identify and prioritize projects to further those ends. Those projects must fit clearly with your college's mission and build on its strengths, have the potential to have an impact on a major portion of the college, and have a group of donors who might support them. One of the major reasons that development efforts fail, both at the college or University level, is a lack of focus—too many projects, projects that are esoteric or grandiose and won't attract support, or projects that aren't exciting and hold little promise to move an institution forward. However difficult prioritizing is, you can only raise private funds for a relatively limited set of projects at any one time. To be successful, you must know your priorities. Only then can you hone your "elevator speech" into a coherent, believable, and persuasive pitch to donors.

So now you are ready with your elevator speech. You and your development officer have practiced giving that speech and have it down cold. Having two to three versions of it, which you can adapt for different audiences, prepares you for unexpected situations and to have more confidence that you can deal with the vagaries of individual donors.

Creating a Development Operation in Arts and Sciences

A development officer within a college of Arts and Sciences, or law, or education, is often referred to as a **constituent officer**, one who represents the constituency of Arts and Sciences faculty, students, alumni, and friends, rather than the University as a whole. The typical argument for creating a Development Office in Arts and Sciences is that it will be closer to the dean and academic departments, more responsive to their needs, and more able to get names of alumni, parents, and friends who are potential donors. This argument is sound. The other crucial role of a constituent development officer in Arts and Sciences is to have someone who works closely with University Development to advance Arts and Sciences' unique needs and communicate with the dean's office on major decisions about donors. The constituent officer, in other words, can be a crucial go-between, internal ambassador, and negotiator between the dean's office and University Development.

The most important questions for you as the new Arts and Sciences dean are who pays for the Arts and Sciences' constituent officer, who hires the person, how is his or her evaluation done, and what are the reporting lines for this person? Many models are possible and are explored more fully in Chapter 3 by Danilowicz and Hayes. At some institutions, the constituent officers are employees of University Development, but assigned to deans with only a "dotted line" responsibility to that dean. The Vice President for Development largely calls the shots. In other systems, deans fund their constituent development officer position, with only a "dotted line" responsibility to the Vice President for Development.

As a dean, you may not have a choice about who hires and evaluates the constituent officer. In any case, get clear who pays and evaluates the person. Regardless of who pays and evaluates, work to ensure that the Arts and Sciences development officer both fully knows and understands your college, but at the same time, is the best ally, confidant, and resource for University Development possible. The ideal situation is that University Development calls your development officer first when there is a problem or an opportunity on the development front having to do with Arts and Sciences. On many gifts, he or she will not be able to take the lead; someone from University Development will. To the extent that the Arts and Sciences development officer can help a University Development officer close a gift for Arts and Sciences successfully, everyone will benefit—Arts and Sciences, University Development, and both development officers. (For more on hiring a development officer, see Chapter 3.)

Can an Arts and Sciences dean create a development effort without hiring an Arts and Sciences development officer? Yes, but in this situation, it becomes incumbent upon the dean to develop a very close working relationship with the Vice President for Development and his/her staff and ensure that they are connecting with the dean's office as they should. In order to have time to make development trips and work with the Development Office, it is usually essential that the dean delegate some duties to an associate or assistant dean. If the dean does not or cannot create an Arts and Sciences Development Office, convincing University Development to designate someone within its ranks to be the liaison with the dean for development in Arts and Sciences may be a crucial step. You should also form close relationships with development officers in University Development and have the backing of the Vice President for Development for these officers to take you along on development visits and to have you review any draft proposal to a donor that is intended to benefit Arts and Sciences.

Development is a Team Sport: The Players

It is critical that you as a dean understand how your University's Office of Development (which may be known as the Advancement Office) is set up. The figure on page 7 depicts a sample organizational chart for a development operation. As depicted in this figure, Development offices have a number of "back office" operations that do not directly raise money. One of the most important is the Research Office that compiles and maintains the data on alumni (or obtains it from the Alumni Office), does research on prospective donors (known as **prospects**), and provides the background information on prospects when a development officer goes out to meet them. If the prospect has been visited before, **contact reports** document the vital information about the interaction: date, place, subject of the conversation, whether there was a gift requested, and so forth. Research provides the background on the prospect and copies the contact reports for the development officer and dean before the next visit.

The other major back office unit in Development is the group that does **stewardship**, i.e., keeping in touch with past donors by inviting them to events, sending annual personal endowment reports, sending

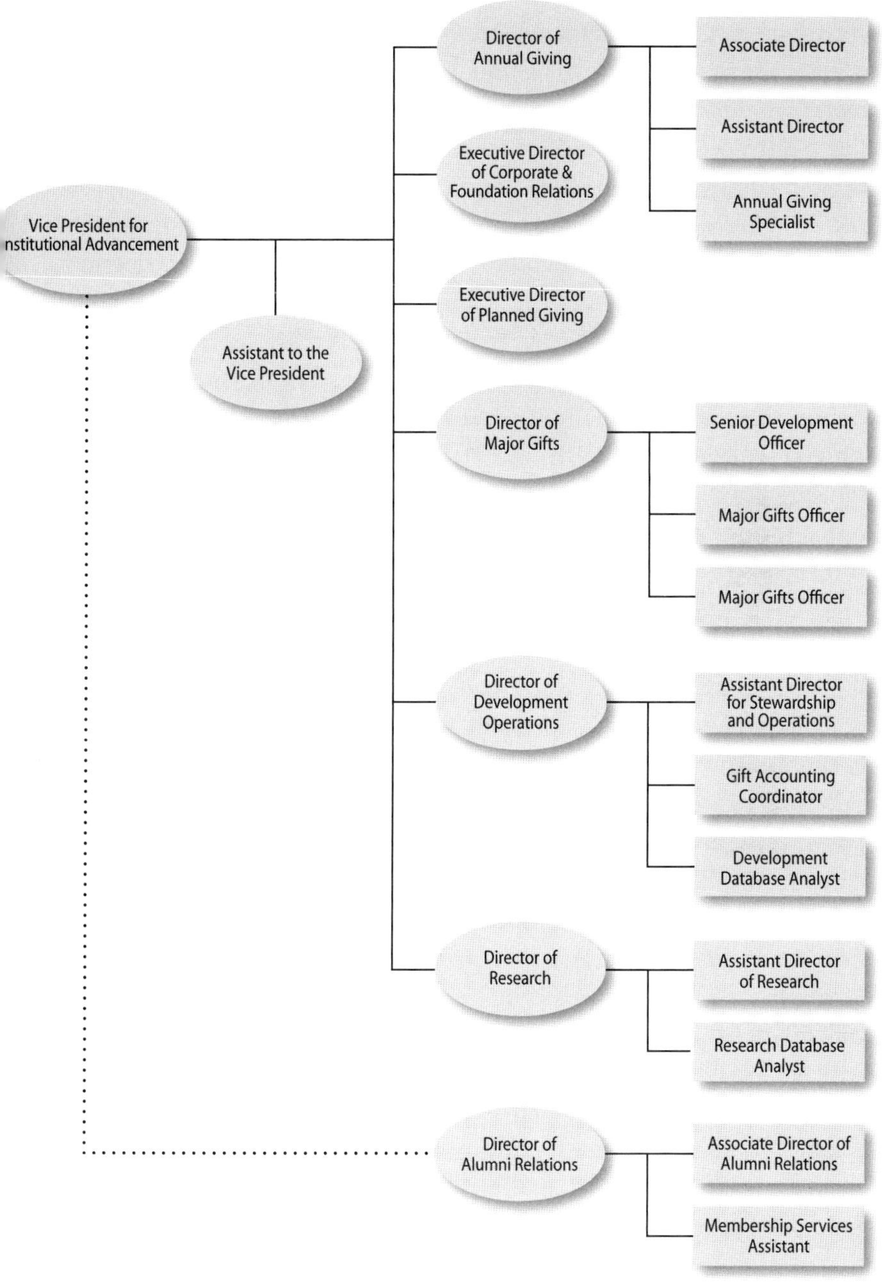

Organization of a Typical University Development Office

contribution thank-you notes, placing plaques on facilities and on donor walls, sending donors' cards on their birthdays, and so forth. A typical name for this operation is **Donor Relations**. The most likely predictor that a prospect will say "yes" to your request is a prior gift, so nurturing these relations is essential—a theme that will be repeated throughout the remainder of this book. All donors should have a positive, even uplifting, experience through their giving.

The Major Fundraising Operations

The typical development operation will have at its core four offices that do direct fund-raising: 1) Corporate and Foundation Relations, 2) the Annual Fund, 3) Major Gifts, and 4) Planned Giving. Each is responsible for different aspects of fund-raising, differentiated by whom they solicit or the form that the gift takes.

Corporate and Foundations Relations (CFR) solicits from companies and private foundations, i.e., not government entities such as the National Science Foundation. Grouping companies and foundations together may seem odd. Many corporations, in the now long ago and lamented days of liberal capitalism, saw philanthropy as a part of their corporate strategy. They often created corporate foundations to make grants or gifts to charity, including higher education. Being good neighbors created good will with governments, local communities, employees, customers, and vendors. Now, corporate philanthropy has declined dramatically; gifts to higher education connect directly to their business and marketing interests.

Despite the change in corporate philanthropy, CFR is still a typical office. An Arts and Sciences Development Office needs to work closely with CFR, or with its private foundation specialist. While the large private foundations such as Ford, Freeman, Gates, Hewlett, Lilly, Luce, Mellon, and Pew can make transformative gifts, some have shifted away from supporting Colleges and Universities, and there is intense competition for what remains of their previous largess to higher education. Your greatest success may come from foundations that you've never heard of, and which people in other parts of the country will never know exist. Every region in the country has regional and local foundations, often called family foundations, which may boast surprisingly large resources. All their gifts, boards of directors, and basic finances are public information, as is their 990 tax information. The CFR person likely is scanning GuideStar and other philanthropic databases to see what other charitable institutions in your area are getting from foundations. Check to see who is on the boards of regional foundations and determine if any of them have ties to your institution and can tell you about the foundations' goals. And, yes, get into the offices of these foundations with the CFR director and find out what intersection there might be between these foundations' interests and your needs. It never makes sense to duplicate in Arts and Sciences what a University Development CFR person is doing centrally. It may make sense to designate an associate or assistant dean to be the liaison with CFR, especially if you're from the sciences and the associate or assistant dean is from the arts, humanities, or social sciences. Just as the Office of Research and Sponsored Programs will usually concentrate on helping the natural and physical sciences in Arts and Sciences get federal grants, so arts, humanities, and social sciences will typically benefit most from CFR's help in getting foundation funding.

The Annual Fund is used to offset institutional operating expenses, by asking alumni, parents, and other friends to give cash gifts each year through direct mail, on-line solicitations, and the tried and true--though increasingly anachronistic—phonathon, an intensive phone-based fundraising campaign, typically is staffed by enthusiastic, lowly paid undergraduate students. The goal is to have these gifts come in as "unrestricted," to be used as the University decides, for the highest need. At many institutions, the annual fund pays for the University Development Office. As crucial as annual fund gifts are for the University, often none or little of this money goes to colleges or schools, a source of endless resentment on the part of deans. As a dean, you cannot be disloyal to the larger institution and undercut the annual fund. At times, remember, besides supporting the University Development Office that helps you raise large gifts, the annual fund in a tight year is all that balances the budget for the University. Nonetheless, frequently, you will have less to do with the Annual Fund Office in terms of raising money

Remainder Unit Trust (CRUT), Retained Life Estate, Lead Trust and Deferred Gift Annuity, etc. You don't need to be an expert in these vehicles though it is helpful to know some of the planned giving jargon. Often transformational gifts such as naming a building will include a variety of giving such as current cash, a gift annuity with an annual payout, and a bequest. Sometimes a Planned Giving Office will have an attorney and/or tax accountant on staff. Few of the wills that name some entity or activity in Arts and Sciences as a beneficiary and are written while you are dean will ever be executed while you are in office. Nonetheless, Planned Giving is a crucial ally. Many people who believe they cannot make a major gift will, however, agree to discuss with the University putting a gift in their will. Once a Planned Giving officer engages with them, they can become more informed and excited about what's going on at the University. A tried and true development strategy is to help a couple or individual write a will benefitting a department or student activity, and then to persuade them to give annually to that beneficiary in order "to begin to see how your funds will make a difference." People of means often find that they don't need as much of their income to maintain their lifestyle as they thought, or they find the satisfaction of giving a joy worth paying for. Once the individual or couple receive glowing letters each year from music students or the chemistry department about the wonderful impact of their annual gift, they frequently decide to give more in order to enjoy the fruits of their philanthropy in their lifetime. Planned Giving officers know, more than anyone, that people give in order to leave a legacy. They are offering prospects a gift just as much as they are soliciting one.

How the Planned Giving officer explains the needs of Arts and Sciences is thus crucial to where these donors direct their funds. Almost no one will ever approach a Planned Giving officer with the goal of benefitting Arts and Sciences. (The exception proves the rule. At one of the institutions where I served, the Arts and Sciences dean will someday enjoy a $250,000 bequest, given by an alumnus who became dean of Arts and Sciences at an Ivy League institution and explained to me that the reason he put Arts and Sciences in his will is because, "If I don't, I know no one else will.") As with the Annual Fund, the Planned Giving officer's knowledge of Arts and Science may be limited, a lacuna made more dangerous because alumni from 60 years ago with whom he or she is working may have a hopelessly out of date view of the University. Indeed, I have seen drafts of bequest agreements that endow a department that Arts and Sciences eliminated decades earlier.

A good Planned Giving officer can teach you other valuable skills: how to work with elderly people and how to work over the long term. As a dean engaged in development, one has to think carefully about a key question: Who has wealth and who is in a position to give it away? In fact, the majority of the major gifts that I have solicited and received came from elderly people. Learning to talk with elderly prospects can take skill and diplomacy. If you have experience with elderly parents, it can be invaluable. All the vagaries of retirement planning, annuities, Florida vacations, Medicare, and, yes, assisted living facilities and nursing homes will become part of your toolkit. Planned Giving specialists are remarkably patient people who learned to develop relationships between the prospect and the institution over years, even decades. On the whole, planned gifts take a much longer time to develop than annual gifts or major gifts.

Whatever name the CFR, Annual Fund, Major Gifts, or Planned Giving go by at your institution, make sure these offices know about the exciting things going on in your college. Take every opportunity to get yourself in front of the University Development staff, especially the MGO's, to tell your story and answer their questions. You want them to see you and your Arts and Sciences development officer as invaluable resources. Keep the Planned Giving officer informed so that he or she can talk knowledgably to those making up their wills about "seeing the fruits of your giving early." And know that students are often the best salespersons for the institution, so long as you explain clearly what their role is and select mature, articulate young people. All donors want to believe that they are shaping the future leaders of America.

Cultivation and Making the Ask

The staff that works so hard on development has one final goal—to raise money, and as much as possible. As the result of careful research, prospects are identified, their interests known and giving capacity estimated. From a variety of sources information is gathered to create a profile of the targeted individual. Contact reports stemming from interaction with the prospect provide updated information that can be used for the "ask."

The first step is to ensure that all the relevant information about the prospect is available—relationship to the University, property ownership, board memberships, known gifts to other charities, media mentions, key civic or religious activities, and so forth. Development officers often start with the assumption that the prospect is interested in either an area in which he or she was involved while at college or that corresponds to their current career or charitable activities. Thus, a biology major who became a doctor and supports the arts might give to the biology department or the pre-med program, or the public health program, or the arts. The hope is that the research process will help to shape a proposal attractive to the donor. I recall a prospect that had graduated as a science major, been an athlete, and become a successful business person, who, initially unbeknownst to us, had become passionate about helping children in a developing part of the world. She ended up making a major gift to help college students do service learning projects during their study abroad in the part of the world she cared about. Only lengthy, thoughtful conversations on the part of the development officer and me elicited this interest and found a way to link her passion with our college's mission.

MGO's develop **moves management strategies** to move a prospect towards making a gift. A move or step might be having the prospect come to campus, having the department chair from the prospect's major visit the prospect, mailing the prospect a signed copy of a noteworthy book published by a faculty member, arranging for the prospect to meet an established donor who supports the college, or having the dean visit. Every contact with a prospect should be tracked by a **contact report** that a development officer files as soon as possible after a visit, phone call, or substantive email. Typically, monthly or quarterly meetings of the Development staff should be held to review the current situation with prospects, mark where they are along a timeline leading to a gift, and recommend a new step—or "move."

Finding the right strategy to bring in a donor is part of the effort; deciding the amount to ask for is the other. Prospects often emerge from **screening,** also known as wealth screening, in which information on whole groups of alumni or other individuals is "screened," without their knowledge, in order to estimate their wealth. Much more can be found in the public record than one might imagine.

The first rule of making the ask is to ask for money. If no one asks, no one is likely to give. It is true that one can ask too early, but the more common fault is not asking. Cultivation should be used to determine the right amount to ask. If prospects who are ready and able to give to Arts and Sciences $100,000 are asked to give $50,000, they usually give $50,000. Do not leave money on the table. Arrive at your best estimate of what is the right number to ask and then go a little higher. Most prospects are flattered that you thought that they might be able to give more than they can. Some will seriously consider giving a higher amount, simply because you asked.

If the first ask fails, after a suitable interval, ask again. Cultivation typically is a lengthy process. Although I once asked a donor for a million dollars on my first meeting and got a commitment for $500,000, that's rare. It only happened because in advance of my visit, University Development had done extensive research on the individual, and a prominent alumnus who had professional ties with the individual had met with him and talked to him about making a gift. As many as seven visits or substantive contacts may be needed before a gift results.

As a busy dean, you should not be making first visits with prospects. After extensive research has been done, MGO's or your Arts and Sciences development officer should be contacting prospects, visiting those that appear to be promising in terms of capacity and interest, and only arranging to have you visit those who are seriously interested.

If you are visiting a prospect for the first time, likely he or she has been visited before by someone at the University, so you will want to read all the contact reports. The bane of many a Vice President for Development and dean is the MGO who puts every possible detail about a prospect into contact reports—pet names, favorite hobbies of children, prospects' proclivities in decorating—but misses crucial clues about wealth or charitable interests. Yet contact reports have to be long and detailed. Often, prospects have to be visited or contacted by multiple staff from the University. Your institution will come off as much more caring if you are not the third person who asks basic information from the prospect. Changes must be made in the University Development database in order to prevent old, inaccurate information in a contact report from misleading the next person who visits the prospect. This is one area in which the Research Office of University Development is critical. Divorces, job changes, promotions, marriages of children, major health issues, other charitable commitments—there is almost nothing of significance about a prospect that is not helpful to know. A good development officer has eyes worthy of Sherlock Holmes. My officer and I had dinner with a prospect whose level of wealth was a bit of mystery to us. I discerned no clues over a pleasant dinner, and we said goodbye to the prospect. But as we walked back towards our hotel, the following exchange occurred:

> DEVELOPMENT OFFICER: "Looks like he's doing well."
> DEAN: "Really? How do you know?"
> DEVELOPMENT OFFICER: "You didn't see his key chain when he laid it on the table with his iPhone?"
> DEAN: "No."
> DEVELOPMENT OFFICER: "His key chain was for a Porsche."
> DEAN: "Really? Wow. Thanks."
> DEVELOPMENT OFFICER: "I get paid to do this."

Cultivation can involve delicate diplomacy. Prospects can have strong views to the right or left of the political spectrum, be deeply religious or outspokenly agnostic, and harbor old resentments about what an instructor, coach, or dean of students did or did not do decades earlier. If you have strong views leave them at home. It is better to be in the center with donors. Prospects can also, without even realizing it, still see the college as the place they knew at twenty-one. While society around them has changed with breathtaking speed, they still imagine their alma mater as a place where students wear bell bottoms or freshmen beanies. One prospect still resented what she perceived as a lack of appreciation for her talents as a female student in the 1970s. For her, giving to the University meant supporting the repression she had experienced. But bringing her back to campus to meet the dynamic women students, faculty, and administrators there in the twenty-first century convinced her to give to the college as a way to support women, not to endorse what she had experienced.

It's not only the prospect herself who may be the key to a gift. The prospect's spouse or partner can be a crucial person in the discussion about giving, even though the prospect has all the wealth. As one college president, who is a champion fundraiser, put it: some of his best donors "were adopted, walked on, or married in." I have met a fair number of couples, usually with the husband as the person with the high income or accumulated wealth, where the husband relies on his wife to make the crucial decisions on philanthropy, including to his alma mater or at least to which aspect of his alma mater that they will contribute.

Non-alumni form a significant portion of giving to colleges and universities. Business leaders who hire your graduates can be generous donors. Parents sometimes identify more with the institution that their children attended than with their alma mater. This is particularly true when the parents, a generation earlier, chose to attend a college simply because it was nearby or the cheapest alternative. They became much invested in their children's college because they spent two years helping choose it and became deeply involved in it through their son or daughter. A parents' council can be a wonderful source of prospects and donations. Grandparents, too, can be very generous. Look for them at senior recitals, final home games, departmental honors receptions, and commencements. Let them take all the photos with you that they want, get their names if you can, and ask them to send you copies of the photos so you get their emails. Usually that's enough for a good research department to do its work.

When making an ask, be well prepared, know that you have earned the right to make the ask with the prospect, listen carefully, and remember that the conversation should be donor centered. Consider setting the stage by planting a seed with your prospect. After telling a story about a specific need, remember to listen for the prospect's response. If the response is favorable you might ask, "Would you be willing to consider supporting this need?" Most people are willing to consider supporting a project that interests them if the timing is right. Also, once you make an ask of any kind, let there be silence that the donor fills with their words. If you receive a negative response, know that no does not necessarily mean no for every request. Donors at first may say no and then call back in six months to reopen the conversation.

While there is clearly an art and a science to fundraising, the magic is in bringing donor interests together with institutional needs. View fundraising as an exciting realm, full of possibilities. The outcome will be that you are helping people to do good things with their largess in support of a noble cause.

Proposals and Gifts

You can ask for a gift and the donor can say yes, but, you and the donor have not really reached an agreement until he or she sees a written **proposal**, agrees to it, and then signs the proposal to indicate acceptance. It is often appropriate to ask a prospect if they "will consider making a major gift to X aspect of the college or University, without naming an amount. If the prospect indicates a positive attitude, you can say that you'll get the prospect a proposal. No matter how enthusiastic the verbal acceptance might be, getting the terms in writing is crucial. The written proposal is the means to do that.

There are different strategies for proposals. Some development offices prefer long, elaborate proposals over which donors and development officers can negotiate at length. Once agreement is reached on the proposal, a pledge form or letter of gift seals the deal. I prefer proposals of no more than one or two pages that make the case for the importance of the gift and name a specific amount and naming opportunity, for example, The Marilyn '61 and Samuel '60 Van Den Berg Fund for Faculty and Student Research. If the prospect agrees to the gift, he or she can sign the proposal indicating acceptance. The proposal is an excellent stage at which the donor finalizes his or her preferences on the amount, the activity she or he wishes to fund, restrictions on the gift, and the like. It is not a legal document, so this allows negotiations between the donor and the college or University to get worked out ahead of time. Then signing the legal document is a formality. Major gifts to name an office or classroom may require a simple pledge card that can be signed at the end of your meeting. Remember that 80 percent of the gifts to higher education are "restricted," that is, they go for specified purpose or aspect of the institution. As the dean, find out the protocol your University's Development Office uses, learn it, and stick with it.

Avoid accepting gifts that will actually cost the University money, known as "gifts that go on taking." My favorite example is a dean with a wealthy donor who wanted to make a major gift to support the teaching of a certain Asian language. The money would have supported one position. But the donor wanted the language position to be the foundation for broader teaching on that part of Asia. The University offered no major for which this language would have been an appropriate complement, and the only way to have an effective Asian studies program around this language would have been hiring faculty in related fields of political science, history, and religious studies. These departments had other needs and did not see teaching on this part of Asia as a high priority. Like this dean, in these situations you're confronted with trying to persuade the donor to broaden or alter the terms of the gift, or convincing the provost and Vice President for Development that you have to turn the gift down. This example points out why it is absolutely essential that the proposal for any major gift intended for your college be seen by you or your development officer before it goes in front of a prospect.

Prospects will sometimes ask for control over a gift. This is something that a charitable organization cannot and must not give. A gift is a gift. Your institution's status as a 501c(3) charitable tax-exempt organization depends on not allowing people to "give" you money, get a tax deduction, and then control the funds in the institution's accounts. If a foundation or company wants to specify how its money is to be used, then they should give a grant, not a gift. Typical contentious issues involve having the donors help select students for scholarships, chose faculty for professorships, and dictate course content for classes in an endowed program. Donors can specify—ahead of time—the purpose their funds will support, the name on the fund or building or portion of the building, and the types of students eligible for their scholarship support. It is important to keep language flexible so that funding is not held captive by a narrow focus. Consider using language such as "with preference given to a student from Pennsylvania." Working out these preferences is crucial, so, again, the proposal and how it is revised is an essential step.

University Development Offices will likely encourage you to ask for an annual fund gift as part of the multiyear capital commitment. This is called a dual ask. The purpose of this is to ensure that when moving a donor up in their giving that it is not at the expense of the annual fund.

Once a prospect has agreed to give her or his funds and thus turns from a prospect into a donor, the **letter of gift (LOG)** becomes the operative document. The LOG is a legal document which should have all the standard language committing the college or University to spending or investing the donation according to IRS regulations, with the usual clauses that will take effect if the activity being helped no longer exists in the future. LOG's are critical because, years in the future, they may be looked at carefully by deans, department chairs, provosts, auditors, and attorneys in order to determine whether or not the terms of the gift were carried out or if the terms will allow a slight change in how the college or University has used the funds.

Stewardship, Alumni Relations, and Communications

Once a gift has been made, the donor falls into the **stewardship** category. Stewardship involves recognizing the donors appropriately in publications or online communications, continuing to communicate with them by mail, making occasional visits, noting significant life events such the marriage of children, retirements, changes of residence, and inviting them to events. Good development operations calibrate the level of stewardship to the level of gift, with the inevitable reality that some very generous donors eschew almost all contact and some donors have an insatiable appetite for attention. (I know of one donor who has given $1.5 million to one of the institutions I've worked for who never wants visits, and tolerates only one mailing a year, and one, amazingly brief, annual phone call). More typically, you will send holiday cards to the same people whom you invite to receptions and major talks on campus and whom you occasionally see on development visits.

Stewardship is critical because the most likely predictor that a prospect will give is that they have given before. You never want to begin cultivating a past donor for a new gift and learn they feel that little attention has been paid to them since their last gift. For Arts and Sciences, as for most constituencies at a University, the lion's share of the stewardship should be done by University Development through its Donor Relations department. It is important to have your Arts and Sciences development officer or a University Development MGO who is assigned to Arts and Sciences, go over the stewardship plan for the most important donors to Arts and Sciences and be reassured that the current strategy reaches out to them as frequently and at the right level as deemed appropriate for that donor.

Stewardship is intimately bound up with alumni relations at the University; an Arts and Sciences dean has to depend on alumni relations being done well at the University level. Donors who have given to Arts and Sciences will continue to receive messages and invitations from alumni relations. It is critical to see that a good working relationship develops between Arts and Sciences and the Alumni Office or Association. Wonderful ways to recognize donors are to have the Alumni Association honor them with an award, or nominate them for search committees, honorary degrees, and so forth. If at all possible, a dean should encourage the Alumni Office to have distinguished, articulate Arts and Sciences faculty members speak to alumni chapters. Encourage academic departments to communicate with their alumni and hold social events around special occasions such as homecoming or reunion.

A dean trying to create an active development effort in Arts and Sciences needs to be aware of and strategically involved in alumni relations. But an Arts and Sciences dean can never hope to build a true alumni-relations operation. The hard truth is that, for development purposes, a strong alumni operation could be wasted effort. A large proportion of your donors will be alumni. But the vast majority of alumni, even those who donate to the University, will not be major donors. Indeed, it is often the case that major donors and alumni leaders are two distinct groups. Most major donors are not inclined to take time from their busy careers or their philanthropic activity to get involved in a local alumni chapter or the Alumni Association, or even to attend homecoming. Typically, only a few Alumni Association leaders are major donors. Nonetheless, the Alumni Office can play a useful role in communicating information about Arts and Sciences, in honoring prominent alumni, and encouraging **annual giving**, that is, cash gifts given each year, and **planned gifts**, a bequest or estate gift given through a will.

Communications is a crucial support for development. It also poses a major decision for an arts and sciences dean. Should you set up your own communications operation within Arts and Sciences or rely on the central administration's Communications Office? The University Communications Office—whether it's called University Relations, Marketing and Communications, or something else—is the single most important outlet for getting out your story from Arts and Sciences to prospective donors. If you and University Development can get University Communications Office to run stories on your highest needs, you have ready-made handouts to use with prospects.

While Arts and Sciences may never have a full-service communications effort, most of the deans who have been successful at development also have had some kind of communications efforts—ranging from a half-time media specialist to a several-person office with a director. One critical area for such a staff person to begin with is the departmental websites for Arts and Sciences. Typically, University communications controls the content management system and the template for all sites on campus, but the actual content is under your control, and it presents a major source of information for development. Every department or interdisciplinary program site should be updated with an eye to what a prospective donor might think. I have told prospects about wonderful things that a department was doing with students, and been met with the reply, "That's funny, their website doesn't make them sound like that at all." Back in my hotel room, I checked the department site and found it horribly out of date, focused on scholarly issues for other academics, or almost completely devoid of news about working with students.

As Steve Otto, the veteran Communications Director in Arts and Sciences at the College of William and Mary used to say repeatedly, "Every department website should have a great story about a student, a faculty member, and an alum, and the story about the student should have faculty member in it, the one about the faculty member should have one or more students in it, and the one about an alum has to mention having worked with a faculty member." Prospects are looking for what it is we say we care about the most—close interactions between faculty and students. Yet, academics can be amazingly insular about what they put on their departmental websites, focusing on faculty scholarship, what they think their academic counterparts at other institutions want to read, or department business—faculty meetings, grant deadlines, and turning in advising schedules. Prospects, like potential students, want to hear about innovative work that students are doing with faculty members, how departments are planning for the future, and success stories about how faculty members helped shape alumni's careers and lives. A good development or Communications Officer can help departments re-shape their messages on websites and ensure that there is always a prominent link: "Want to help more great students and faculty like this? CLICK HERE."

What Not to Do: Event Planners, Lone Rangers, and Crying Poor

Why are some Arts and Sciences development offices unsuccessful in raising funds? Three common mistakes are: first, having your Development Office become mired in planning events and doing alumni relations; second, allowing individual faculty members or departments go off on their own to try to raise money—the Lone Ranger phenomenon; and, third, trying to raise money by "crying poor," i.e., telling prospects about the imminent failure of Arts and Sciences and its departments, rather than their successes, as a way to encourage donations.

Wisely organized receptions, lunches, dinners, get-togethers for guest speakers on campus—all of these have a place in development. If you can get a group of prospects together in one place at one time, you or a development officer can make lots of connections quickly and inexpensively. These are also good acts of stewardship. Used properly, such events can also let the dean lay out the need for a major new initiative such as a building project or a faculty-student research program. As part of arranging for these events, and as stewardship, the dean or the Arts and Sciences development officer has to do a certain amount of alumni relations. The danger is that this kind activity—event planning and connecting with alumni—becomes an end in itself. Success becomes measured in how many people turned up at an event or how many responses Arts and Sciences received to its last newsletter to supporters or a similar metric. Development officers, particularly constituent officers who are not surrounded by other development colleagues, can become distracted from their goal: asking prospects for money and getting some of them to say "yes."

Another danger arises when the dean introduces a fundraising goal to his or her department chairs, asks them for the names of alumni who might have financial capacity, and urges them to draw up their priorities. Which may lead the chair to wonder, "Why wait for the dean or some over-worked MGO to contact the alum when I can call and ask her directly for $10,000 to buy that piece of equipment that the vice provost for research is being so stingy about?" Department chairs and faculty usually have to have development strategy explained to them. Donors dislike being treated like a check book or a piggy bank to be raided when needed. They also dislike multiple requests of widely varying amounts. If the department chair asks for $10,000, the donor will assume that the needed piece of equipment is the highest priority of Arts and Sciences, and he may well give the $10,000. When the dean comes to visit the next week and says that the highest priority of Arts and Sciences is the new program in service learning to which the dean would like the donor to give $250,000, the donor will resent having been asked for the $10,000. You always want to give clear, consistent signals to prospects that you have your priorities straight, that you're avoiding multiple or gratuitous asks, and that the prospect is a special person whom you're presenting with an important opportunity to help the college.

Another reason to keep the Lone Rangers reined in, or at least well-trained on the ranch, is that they are quick to persuade prospects that private funds are needed to avert some imminent disaster—cutting upper division classes, conference travel, or departmental lecture funds. Crying poor rarely interests donors. Donors like to give to success, not to prevent collapse. Also, while it may come as a shock to hardworking faculty members struggling to get by on modest salaries, many prospects, even those who believe strongly in the value of higher education, tend to believe faculty members have it pretty good. The imminent disaster of reduced conference travel might provide the material for a good joke at the country club. Faculty members, after all, have privileges few private sector employees possess: scheduling much of their own time during the typical work week, deciding what they want to research or which grants to pursue, participating in choosing their supervisor (i.e., chair), and having at least three months of vacation each year. And did I mention tenure? Most donors understand that faculty members have their freedom because they work with students and create and carry on knowledge. Prospects and donors often have little patience for tales of faculty deprivation. Faculty members may have to be coaxed to tell stories about the great things that students are doing with faculty members and how, with a major gift or greater annual giving, prospects can help us have an even greater impact on young people's lives.

These common mistakes—event planning and alumni relations run amuck, Lone Rangers, and crying poor—explain why many Vice Presidents of Development are wary of constituency development offices. Too many constituency officers, as is said in many a University Development Office, "go native." That is, they identify with the immediate interests of their constituency and fail to get the dean and his or her faculty to adopt a culture of development that promotes the long-term interests of the institution. It is also true that Arts and Sciences is renowned among development officers for having the worst internal battles over what to raise money for and how to best to raise it. Regardless of their knowledge about the subject (or lack thereof), Arts and Sciences faculty members generously share their advice on how fundraising should be done. As Mark Roche, the longtime dean of

Arts and Sciences at the University of Notre Dame put it, "A dean is the conductor of an orchestra made up entirely of composers." Development officers can easily get sucked into trying to referee inter-departmental battles or in reining in the Lone Rangers. One Vice President told me that in his experience, it took at least a year after a constituency development officer moved back to University Development for the officer to get back to a higher level of effectiveness as a fundraiser. To avoid distraction from the main goal, an Arts and Sciences dean and development officer needs to work closely with University Development, listen to their advice, and be aware that the dangers are real. With good professional advice, a clear message from the dean that development is essential and needs to be run professionally, and a consistent focus on cultivation, proposals, and asks, an Arts and Sciences Development Office can be successful.

The Joy of Giving and Receiving

Despite the potential pitfalls and setbacks, many Arts and Sciences deans and development officers have created successful fundraising operations and raised impressive sums. And, despite the fears, or disdain, that some faculty members have for fundraising, it can be interesting and even fun. Most prospects interested in giving to the College that merit the dean's attention are people with a great deal of life experience, broad tastes, and creative minds that have already given to hospitals, the arts, religious organizations, schools, and political causes. They have a lot to share and much to teach you. Once they see you're not an intellectual elitist, they like hearing about your college's intellectual, artistic, and scientific endeavors. They also appreciate your being a manager, who has had to deal with budget cuts, personnel problems, and strategic planning. They will be your willing partner; they provide the funds and you the expertise and appropriate skills and resources in a cooperative effort to advance the educational mission.

You offer your prospects a chance to make a difference. By working with you, donors can do something with their money that shapes young people's lives, passes on the wisdom of centuries, helps discover new knowledge or create artistic works, and builds an institution that will last for generations. In short, you can help them leave a legacy. As the old Irish saying puts it, "Shrouds have no pockets." Through their gifts, they can create a connection to your students, your institution, and the community of your alumni, parents, and friends. As Nelson Mandela believed, "Education is the most powerful weapon we have to change the world." Together with a good development operation, you and your donor partners can get started on that noble cause.

2

Arts and Sciences on Campus

Matthew C. Moen

Since higher education institutions were established on our shores, the liberal Arts and Sciences have been the intellectual centerpiece of the American University. The Europeans who founded Harvard and the College of William and Mary–the first American universities –were committed to the seven liberal arts of medieval times, usually subdivided into a *trivium* (grammar, rhetoric, logic) and *quadrivium* (astronomy, arithmetic, geometry, music).

Today, many public and private Colleges and Universities reflect this heritage through a freestanding college of Arts and Sciences housing academic departments in the humanities, fine arts, social sciences, and sciences. Of the 500 CCAS institutions, about 60 percent have a dean of Arts and Sciences. Other Colleges and Universities distribute departments among separate colleges of Arts and Humanities, Fine Arts, Social and Behavioral Sciences, and/or Sciences. But no matter the specific structure, the academic departments comprising the liberal Arts and Sciences are the core of the University. A college of Arts and Sciences will typically house somewhere around 50 percent of all undergraduates at a major research University, and an even higher percentage at a residential liberal arts college. Remaining undergraduates and graduate/professional students are usually spread across schools such as agriculture, architecture, business, dentistry, education, engineering, health sciences, law, marine sciences, medicine, or pharmacy.

The importance of Arts and Sciences can be seen in the 2010 Carnegie Foundation for the Advancement of Teaching report that classifies

Arts and Sciences may also compare unfavorably in job placement statistics. Our sheer size makes it difficult to track Arts and Sciences placement vis-à-vis professional schools, and liberal arts graduates tend to gain most of their professional success later in life, rather than right after graduation. The rallying cry of Arts and Sciences tends to be that it is the last job, not the first job that matters most. The traditional message of education for its intrinsic worth to lead a richer, a more reflective, and engaged life is an ideal that seems increasingly muddled amidst the public educational rhetoric favoring careerism.

Finally, professional schools often have a fundraising head start because their donors see it is in their self-interest. Businesses want accountants and hospitals want nurses, so they see a generous donation to a relevant professional school as an investment in their own future well-being; they may even hope for an implicit *quid pro quo* that outstanding graduates will be sent their way. Most departments within the Arts and Sciences lack that type of self-interested sponsorship.

Thus, the dean of Arts and Sciences seeking outside financial support may be likened to a runner starting a race uphill. Yet, the race is rewarding and can be won. A vast potential donor base provides a leg up, as does the centrality of the Arts and Sciences to the mission of any higher education institution. Colleges and Universities with a Phi Beta Kappa chapter will produce graduates likely to be successful and steeped in the liberal Arts and Sciences. To help the new Arts and Sciences dean better understand his/her own point of departure, the rest of this chapter examines the dean's fundraising role within a College or University setting. Typical fundraising models, the dean's relationship with Foundation Development staff, and the dean's position vis-à-vis other University entities and operations will be covered.

Fundraising Models

The most basic fundraising division is a centralized versus decentralized model. This will probably not be the dean's call, but rather is decided by the college or University president in tandem with the head of the Foundation and the Foundation's governing board. The dean usually inherits, and operates within, the structure already established, but he/she may be able to shape it over time. Success begets flexibility.

Smaller institutions almost invariably use a **centralized model**, where the major gift officers and other fundraising staff solicit funds for all projects at the College or University, including all academic programs in the liberal Arts and Sciences. This formula is a straight economy-of-scale issue, where the institution lacks the resources and the need to hire dedicated gift officers for particular academic colleges or schools. Typically in this arrangement, the fundraising staff will be paid out of University or Foundation revenues, depending on whether the Foundation is a separate legal entity.

The fundraising staff will do most of the legwork. They contact donors, solicit gifts, and complete contact reports for donors visited. They likely follow some type of monthly "moves metric" that describes their number of visits and asks for money, and summarizes which people they moved further along toward a major gift. The role of the dean is more of a "closer" of intermediate-size gifts, talking the donor into actually writing the check or signing the transfer of wealth documents. Usually, the campus president and the Foundation president are the closers for the largest gifts to campus. This system tends to stay focused on the largest donors, and offers the distinct advantage of smooth handoffs between the fundraising staff and the closers.

The downside of the centralized model is that the development officer may lack detailed product knowledge. If they are covering the entire College or University, for instance, they need to know about the liberal Arts and Sciences, but also probably business, education, athletics, and still other units. Even within the scope of Arts and Sciences, they may have difficulty explaining in great detail the short-term and long-term needs of the academic programs they are tasked to advance.

The lack of a single person with responsibility for the Arts and Sciences can benefit the dean in the sense that all of the development officers are soliciting gifts from Arts and Sciences alumni. Yet, the situation can also be a disadvantage. The dean may be called upon frequently to explain some pretty basic information about academic departments to different major gift officers who interact with donors and follow up on leads. In this model, the dean lacks a single "go to" person to search out specific gifts, but rather coordinates with a bevy of modestly informed gift officers. The dean can easily lose out to the professional schools, or to athletics, whose missions require much less explanation. At most Colleges and Universities, the principal fundraising conflict for the Arts and Sciences likely will be with athletics because the latter can plausibly claim all alumni as their own.

Larger institutions opt for a **constituency model**, where the development officers are distributed across individual colleges and professional schools. This practical arrangement recognizes that no development officer can plausibly cover the donor base, nor be knowledgeable about the vast academic programming at a major University. At my own University, for instance, a development officer in the college of Arts and Sciences is responsible for understanding twenty-one undergraduate programs, fourteen master's degrees, seven doctoral degrees, numerous service and research centers, and commitments to cross-cutting University goals like retention, mentorship, and diversity. For the largest Universities, the Arts and Sciences are even more bewildering, with as many as forty academic departments in the humanities, social sciences, and sciences. Typically, one or more development officers are assigned to the college of Arts and Sciences, tasked to work closely with the dean. This arrangement has the mirror opposite advantages and disadvantages of the centralized approach. The clear point of contact facilitates communications with a development officer who better understands Arts and Sciences. If the dean shares in the funding of the development officer's salary, there is more opportunity to shape the direction of fundraising.

But constituency fundraising also has drawbacks. Development officers (unless housed in major metropolitan areas where many alumni live in close proximity) struggle to cover the broad swath of territory where their donors reside. The development officer (or for that matter, the dean) is palpably disadvantaged in the sense that a single contribution to some component of Arts and Sciences is less evident to a donor as a way to boost the whole. For example, a gift to accounting or finance is easily viewed as helping the business school as a whole; in contrast, a gift to physics does not help English much, just as a gift to psychology does not help earth sciences or French.

An alternative, given the pros and cons of the centralized versus constituency approach, is the **hybrid model**. It favors constituency fundraising within a planned radius of the home campus, such as the state or region, but then deploys other development officers across the country so that they raise money for all colleges/schools on campus. This allows more cost-efficient visitation of potential donors across the nation. But a hybrid model is no panacea. For the dean, the handoff of potential donors by different development officers can be awkward. The non-constituency development officers may decide quite on their own to focus on some colleges/schools at the expense of others. Less knowledge of Arts and Sciences, or fewer wealthy donors, likely means those operations will end up disadvantaged relative to the professional schools of business, law, and medicine. Development officers operating on the single most important metric of fundraising (how much money is actually brought into the Foundation) have an incentive to gravitate toward the high-end professional school alumni first, because they are the most wealthy graduates and, on average, the most capable donors.

Whatever the fundraising structure, the dean must establish a solid rapport with fundraising staff in the quest for gifts. A good place to start is by looking together at the Council for the Advancement and Support of Education (CASE) Statement of Ethics, originally adopted in 1982 by the CASE Board of Trustees. Designed to apply to advancement professionals, the ethics statement describes high standards of professional conduct. For instance, it calls upon major gift officers to respect privacy and confidentiality, to refuse favors for personal gain, and to avoid conflict-of-interest in the process of raising private dollars; the statement encourages gift officers to promote their institution without denigrating its component parts and to avoid discriminatory behavior.

Beyond the CASE principles, an individual dean may wish to elucidate some of his/her own fundraising principles. Ideas that come to mind are not sacrificing a long-term relationship for a short-term gift. Another is for a development officer (unless otherwise agreed upon) to refrain from making academic promises to donors, such as coming back to campus to teach a class. Common sense and best practices dictate that fundraising staff will arrive prepared and on time to meet with donors.

They will protect the reputation of the liberal Arts and Sciences, promote its programs and its academic goals, and graciously refer prospective donors to other parts of the University, if those more clearly align with the donor's giving interests. They will follow up with donors in timely and appropriate ways.

No matter the theoretical model, when the dean begins fundraising in earnest, most likely the effort will turn into some kind of amalgamation of those ideal-type models. Donors and circumstances do not neatly fit into fundraising models; in that sense, almost every model is some sort of hybrid. And even where some particular model is being followed, it may not be sustained. A typical example would be the dean who starts with a constituency fundraising approach, but gradually morphs it into a hybrid or even more centralized approach, because the University launches a seven-year capital campaign. A dean may start out fundraising for specific departments and liberal arts education, for instance, but then be asked as part of a capital campaign to take a back seat with major donors so they can be asked to support higher priority campus projects. Or the dean may be asked to move from seeking named faculty endowments to finding money for student scholarships. Thus, the prudent dean will invest in personal relationships with donors, rather than be wedded to a particular fundraising model.

Finally, the dean is wise to remember that there will likely be mixed messages about the role they are supposed to play as they interact with presidents, provosts, fellow deans, department chairs, and faculty.

Externally-oriented presidents may expect the deans to assist fundraising efforts or, believing they have the external world in hand, may leave it up to the provost and deans to run the academic side of the shop on campus. More internal campus presidents—rather a disappearing breed—may expect the deans to stay home or, because they don't like fundraising, may expect them to fill that role. Expectations vary by president and over time. In most cases, the provost will be heavily internal and will expect the deans to pay very close attention to their academic shops because that reflects upon academic affairs; the dean tasked to fundraise therefore needs a provost who understands and supports the balancing act, who grasps the tradeoffs. Fellow deans may be competitors or partners. Department chairs tend to think the dean's priority should be on campus talking to them and faculty and students, perhaps teaching some on the side while also keeping up a research program. Department chairs and faculty more highly value the dean who remains the teacher/scholar than the fundraiser, partly because they can see the former activity but not the latter. Without a sense of the work involved in fundraising, the faculty may assume it is a time-sink, or a pretty easy thing to get people to write checks to their alma mater.

Relationship with the Foundation

The relationship between the Arts and Sciences dean and the Foundation is critical to success. To a considerable extent, the key is for both sides to develop a solid understanding of the world the other inhabits.

The development officer, for instance, must know that fundraising is only a small component of a dean's work; what typically occupies the dean are personnel matters, programmatic issues, budget, recruitment and retention, and then as time permits, fundraising and alumni relations. The vastness of an Arts and Sciences college requires much more internal governance and communication than a professional school. To cite but one example, a dean of a professional school probably has all of his/her faculty in a single building; the Arts and Sciences dean has departments in multiple buildings, perhaps a dozen or more. And then beyond the size difference, the Arts and Sciences dean likely will be caught up more in related campus conversations, such as space utilization, recruitment of first-year students, scholarship administration, web site traffic, and retention. Other than commenting on how well it prepares students, professional schools like law or medicine seldom participate in discussions about general undergraduate education. They are not responsible for the delivery or quality of the writing, math, science, and speech classes that are the core of a student's first year in college. They do not face remedial education issues or the scope of readmission cases for students who start college on the wrong foot.

The development officer needs to appreciate that a dean puts in long hours, many of which are relatively intense. A dean may wish to carve out a small amount of space for his/her own professional, disciplinary activities, mindful of a possible return to the faculty at a future time. Deans do not wish to "cold call" prospective donors because it is an inefficient use of their time. They do not like to fundraise in distant places without some hope for tangible success because their work load back home grows while they are away. They prefer to fundraise around events they are already planning to attend, such as professional conferences. They place some of the fundraising priorities higher than others, often favoring donor gifts to current funds that help current students and faculty, rather than favoring bequests or other promises of future gifts. This is especially true if the Foundation or the provost unwisely employ some set of metrics that invites immediate fundraising results, rather than taking a long-term approach.

The development officer must also understand and value the dean who is able to speak often and elegantly about the liberal Arts and Sciences. Here the dean occupies a unique role on the campus, and one of the best things he/she can do to facilitate fundraising is to promote the liberal Arts and Sciences, especially if a constituency fundraising model is being used.

In turn, the dean needs to understand the world the development officer inhabits. The development officer lives in a world of imperfect data. This leads to many false leads for the gift officer and the dean. A key element for fundraising is estimating the wealth of potential donors. And central to that estimate is the prospect's home address and neighborhood. But that data is sometimes misleading. People can show up in a database as wealthy when the reality is that their discretionary money is tied up in their home. Because of the high market value of single family homes in desirable areas people typically appear wealthy. What the database does not show is their high mortgage payments over the course of several decades, perhaps with a balloon payment at the end, or other constraints on their apparent income. A dean I know showed up for dinner at a restaurant in a posh community where she expected to meet with a wealthy donor, based on database estimation of wealth. The dean was taken aback when the donor pulled up in an old, high-mileage car. In the course of polite conversation, the donor circled around to the fact that he lived in a lovely home in a tony residential area, but that most of his accumulated wealth and discretionary income went with his three previous wives. In the Foundation database, he showed up as an elderly, single man with genuine giving potential. After a meal at which the dean initially hoped to secure a major gift, she left with a personal check from the donor for $125. Lesson learned: wealth estimation based on real estate often does not tell the whole story.

Development officers work under pressure. They may knock on ten doors, only to have eight shut on them, and so the constant work of finding donors willing to have a conversation is time-consuming. The development officer feels the same time demands, office politics, and organizational imperfections that any professional tries to negotiate. One particular worry is doing a great deal of the heavy lifting with a donor (getting them to think philanthropically) only to have a major gift leach out to another person or another cause outside of constituency fundraising. Still another worry is striking the proper balance, making sure the dean is not bothered with extraneous fundraising matters, while trying to ensure a dean is in on any major gift that develops for Arts and Sciences since that involvement helps cement donor relations. The dean must always be sensitive to the development officer's need for substantial credit since the amount of money raised is their ultimate metric.

The dean must also understand the metrics of development. The Foundation may track a development officer's total visits per month and per year. The Foundation may use a complex reporting system of "moves management" that tracks precisely how well the development officer is moving prospective donors along toward a major gift. A development officer is actively managing a portfolio of dozens and dozens of prospective donors, with a fairly standard number being 150 donors. Some of those donors will require quite a bit of attention. The officer is busy writing up contact reports of prior visits, saying what happened, while also strategically planning future visits. The officer is thinking about raising money all across the Arts and Sciences, not just in a few departments. He/she will also be thinking about the balance between raising current funds and establishing long-range endowments.

The driving metric is actual dollars brought into the Foundation.

A development officer can do all of the data analysis in the world. He/she can find donors and meet with them, and the gift officer can do a wonderful job of communicating and following up with donors who have given previously. But if he/she does not succeed in bringing money into the Foundation, it does not equal success. For that reason, the development officer may need to close gifts now rather than get a bigger gift later; the officer may be willing to push donors a bit outside Arts and Sciences if it sounds like the giving potential is greater elsewhere because he/she will likely receive some credit for the amount received, regardless of its destination. These types of cross-pressures are no greater for gift officers than for deans, but are a more consistent presence in the daily job.

In an ideal world, the Foundation compiles solid data and provides an initial vetting of a prospective donor. It resolves the conflicts that arise among development officers with regard to region, college or school, or specific donors. It liberates the dean to ask for substantial gifts, having provided training for those who require it. In return, the dean offers a personal presence when he/she is truly needed, requiring time and travel. Ideally, the dean also provides ongoing stewardship of past donors, since they remain the most likely future contributors. Finally, the dean engages in personal, ongoing professional development. Obvious choices to increase a dean's skill set are the fundraising seminars offered episodically by the Council of Colleges of Arts and Sciences, the Council for the Advancement and Support of Education, and the Association of Fundraising Professionals. A less obvious choice is participating in the Women's Philanthropy Institute on the campus of Indiana University–Purdue University in Indianapolis (IUPUI). Still another option is the endless array of webinars offered by all types of non-profit and for-profit organizations; a simple Google search turns up more than one million hits for the phrase "fundraising webinars." Reading this book is a step in the right direction. (Appendix A includes additional resources.)

The Broader Campus

Arts and sciences deans interact with department chairs, other deans and a provost and/or vice president of academic affairs. From both chairs and provosts, the dean needs understanding of the fundraising obligation, which only grows when the effort is successful, because it increases the task of donor stewardship. Normally this relationship will be fairly straightforward with the provost because he/she will realize the dean's time commitment to the task and will probably not have many competing fundraising priorities. Deans share many of the same kind of responsibilities. The department chairs present a more complicated situation.

Just as the dean wants to direct gifts into the Arts and Sciences, a chair has the incentive to book gifts into his/her own department. If presented with the opportunity, chairs may be willing to steer donors more narrowly than the dean. They may be willing to sacrifice the size of a gift for the precise location of a gift; this is akin to the Arts and Sciences dean who would rather have a gift to the college of $100,000 than a gift to some other entity of $105,000. As a group, department chairs will embrace fundraising with varying degrees of enthusiasm. Some will very much want to lay groundwork for donations by reaching out to alumni, with successes usually facilitating more effort; some chairs may even be interested in pointedly asking their alumni for donations, or at least providing good leads for the gift officer and dean. Other chairs are not much interested in soliciting money from people they helped educate, perhaps to the point of finding the whole fundraising enterprise a bit distasteful.

As seen in the example below, departments that embrace fundraising can benefit immensely from the effort.

> Fundraising for the Department of Portuguese began with a faculty member who carefully mentored undergraduates over a period of many years. Later on, she contacted a few of her former students who she knew did quite well financially to see if they would be willing to contribute to an endowment set up at the Foundation just for the department. Some initial contributions rolled in, creating momentum to go back out to other prospective donors and invite them to join. A flood of donations followed, with individual contributors giving because of the accomplished mentor or because

graduates will not overlap, but the wealthiest Arts and Sciences alumni likely ended up owning or running a business. If the business school consistently approaches them on that basis, rather than on their undergraduate major, conflict ensues. Solid communication must occur with Arts and Sciences and business to avoid difficulty; in most cases, this means respectful solicitation that allows a donor to choose. The advantage the Arts and Sciences dean has is that donors may believe their liberal education was the ticket to their business success; the disadvantage is that donors who succeed in business are so used to talking money that they might establish a better rapport with the business dean who occupies their world than with the Arts and Sciences dean who is grounded in linguistics or computational chemistry.

Other professional schools present fewer issues. The professional schools usually associated with the historic land-grant University (agriculture, architecture, engineering, forestry, and marine sciences) tend to produce alumni with disparate earning potential. Those in engineering or architecture may fare well, while the average agriculture graduate may not. But the larger point is that, apart from general education, these graduates do not intersect much with Arts and Sciences during their college matriculation. Usually there is no reason for them to wish to support the Arts and Sciences financially. Conflict related to fundraising rarely ensues.

Professional schools of education and health sciences present contrasting situations. Education produces secondary school teachers with a healthy dose of Arts and Sciences in a content area, but with few opportunities for wealth accumulation if their graduates remain teachers throughout their careers (occasional exceptions are the tight-fisted or the dual-career couple). The fundraising task with school of education graduates is to filter them carefully for giving capacity because in most cases it will be quite limited; it is a task that falls to the school of education fundraising operation. Similar circumstances may exist with undergraduates in the health sciences, but those with completed graduate degrees may be quite well positioned to contribute. Jurisdictional or donor conflict with Arts and Sciences is more likely to happen with education than with health sciences.

Outside of the academic hierarchy of department chairs, college deans, provost, and president, few on campus probably give fundraising much thought. Other than some occasional interaction with visiting donors, faculty are not tasked to fundraise. Neither are support offices like Human Resources, IT, Marketing, and Admissions. The Graduate School or Office of Research may wish to be involved with donors, but those tend to be administrative structures that process applications or grants, without too much faculty or donor allegiance. Student Affairs focuses almost exclusively on current students, not on giving by future alumni. Most classified employees on campus lack any type of connection to fundraising.

A notable exception to the general lack of interest in fundraising is the University Alumni Association. Its ability to keep alumni engaged in the life of a University is critical, especially if the departments are unable to sustain that contact for lack of ability or desire. The Alumni Association communicates regularly, hosts events, and raises money in modest amounts to support its operations. It sells University merchandise. It promotes attendance at athletic and other University events. More than any other entity, it rallies the faithful to attend and participate in homecoming, which is a special time when former graduates often reconnect with their alma mater. The Alumni Association is understandably sensitive that its scheduled events remain comparatively free of direct monetary appeals, but its events can be instrumental in laying the groundwork for the Foundation's later successful fundraising.

Conclusion

The liberal Arts and Sciences occupy a central place in the intellectual life of a college or University. Especially at a residential, private College, Arts and Sciences will be the focal point of fundraising; at even the nation's largest research universities, the Arts and Sciences will have a claim and major stake in fundraising. And yet, as we have pointed out, the Arts and Sciences face unique challenges raising money for their students, faculty, and academic programs. Fundraising is best viewed as a work always in progress.

Simply getting started within the structure provided by a University is the first step for a dean. As much as anything, this probably means a genuine embrace of fundraising as an important activity. Arts and Sciences deans tend to be steeped in the culture of teaching and research, rather than finances, so this can be a mental adjustment. And carving out time is challenging, given the relentless demands of the dean's other responsibilities.

Slow, tangible progress may be the best possible outcome in Arts and Sciences for the dean who is completely new to fundraising. Yet successful fundraising will be among a dean's most enduring and important accomplishments. Long after committee meetings are forgotten and personnel matters are resolved, permanent endowments assist students and faculty. Long after the vagaries of middle management dissipate, permanent endowments keep the institution strong.

3

Organizing the Dean's Office for Development

Bret S. Danilowicz and Julie C. Hayes

In your role as dean, likely you walked into a pre-existing structure for development in your office. But is this structure the one that best serves your college? Your office may have been operating with certain roles and activities because it suited the personality or priorities of a previous dean. You are a unique individual and will have different goals than the previous college administration. As you read this chapter, we encourage you to take a fresh look at your office's development structure, and to update responsibilities and operations to make fundraising more effective and meaningful for your college.

Your office will be building lasting relationships between alumni and other supporters with your departments, the College and the University; these relationships should not depend upon you or your development officer. You will likely find that development officers come and go with a startling frequency (the same can be said for deans at many institutions), and if the development relationship has been tailored to an individual in your office, you have done your college a great disservice when that individual departs.

Development Responsibilities

Previous chapters provide insight into the role of the dean and development officer in fundraising efforts. Here, we will deepen your understanding of the responsibilities associated with these respective roles, but also lay out related duties of other individuals in your office, along with those of one or more external (advisory) boards. You may be new to the development process; do not forget that it also may be new to others in your office. Not every development officer starts with fundraising experience, and not every job description for staff or department chairs refers to development responsibilities (although you are encouraged to add these at your first opportunity). Development should be discussed and adjusted with your office team to achieve buy-in and to optimize their role, as appropriate for you and your institution.

Dean

Above all, the dean's development responsibilities are to set the development goals and strategy for the college. As Strikwerda writes in the opening chapter, it is easiest to build upon a strategic plan if one is available for your college, and if not, a list of the college's key strengths and related top-needs will work. To help turn prospective donors into major donors, your vision for development must have enticing yet attainable goals. Listing grandiose projects, for which you do not have the donor base, projects for which funding should really be supplied by the campus (as for building maintenance), or ones with hurried completion times, will not position your office for success.

> *(BSD)* When I started as dean, the former dean had promised to support a department with a large sum of cash for student travel. No money and no likely donors were in hand, yet the students had been planning this trip for a full year and already had press coverage. While I was loath to 'eat' this expense, due to the time it would have taken to raise the necessary funding, I decided to charge it to other parts of the college budget. We used our development time to secure other gifts for the college—a more promising start to a deanship.
>
> *(JCH)* I, too, found myself faced with a development effort from a previous administration: a multi-million dollar capital project spearheaded by an individual faculty member, a "Lone Ranger," as Strikwerda described them in Chapter 1. The project—conceptually exciting, but a low priority for the University—had attracted one major gift and many small

donations, but not nearly enough to move ahead. Other major prospects had evaporated. My development officer and I have exercised much careful diplomacy to work with the major donors (and the Lone Ranger) to demonstrate stewardship of the earlier gift, while pointing the way towards alternative means of realizing their intent.

Your strategic plan's development priorities should be shaped in concert with department chairs and faculty; you need their support for your time associated with development. You will need to set a goal for how much of this funding should be targeted for endowments and for the competing category of expendable cash. In the context of a campaign, you will need a range of options at different giving levels, from capital projects and endowed professorships to current-use scholarship funds, projects, or equipment. Giving levels for naming opportunities may need to be approved by a central Development Office. While donors will ultimately decide where their money goes, based on your objective, your development officer and marketing staff will guide their conversations towards supporting immediate projects or long-term endowments.

Your college's development strategy will include getting alumni and friends (henceforth collectively referred to as 'alumni') to become engaged with college activities towards annual giving and culminating in providing major gifts (see figure on page 50). Alumni engagement creates a pool of potential donors who may become annual donors in the short term. Investing time on alumni engagement is a tradeoff with 1) time to develop donors who are able to support the college now with major gifts, and 2) time for stewardship which encourages major and even annual donors to give again. How much time you and your development officer spend in each activity will depend on institutional support for these activities outside the college (e.g. an Alumni Association office), and the cash versus endowment needs for the college. The strategy you select for your development officer depends upon whether you or someone outside the college is the direct supervisor.

Beyond stipulating your development officer's use of time, you are also responsible for protecting that time. You may be surprised to see

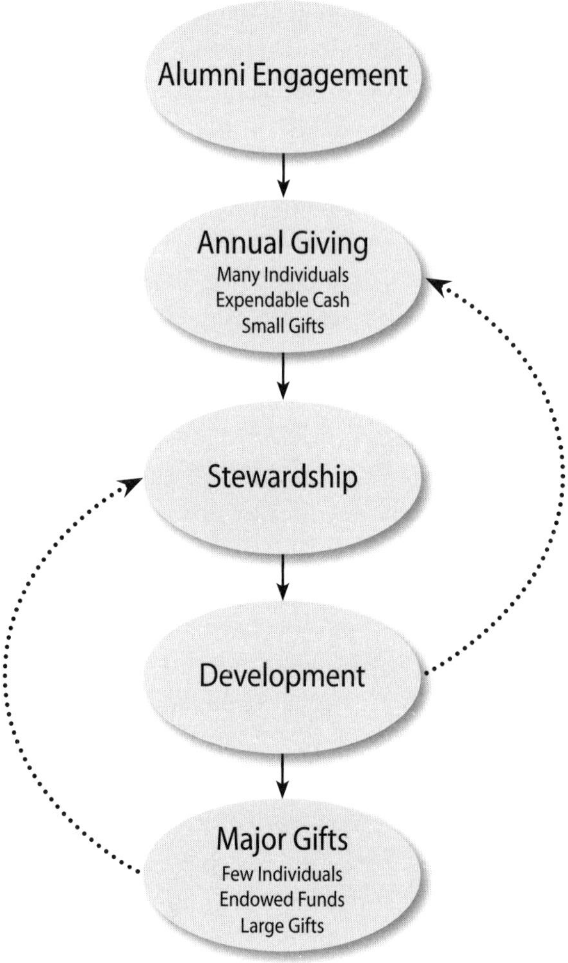

Engaging Your Alumni

Engaging alumni will increase the number that provide annual gifts to the college. Through stewardship then continued development, individuals giving annual gifts can be converted into major donors for the college.

the number of requests for assistance that will land on your development officer's desk: annual giving, the Alumni Association, college and department advisory boards, your communications team (for newsletters and magazines), homecoming committees, department chairs … the list goes on! The more time your development officer spends on tangential activities, the less time spent cultivating donors. Your development officer is likely to encounter conflicts where another college or athletics lay claim to particular donors. Since you are much more likely to have established relationships with these other units, it is best if you resolve these cases for the college as they arise and avoid putting your officer in an awkward situation.

As described in Chapter 2, Arts and Sciences is a complex college, and you will have alumni-rich and alumni-poor departments, both in numbers and in gift potential. You need to determine the strategy for working among departments. You and your development officer will tend to be drawn where the money is; the University and your marketing staff will love to tout large gifts. However, by supporting only "rich" departments, the others will become disenchanted with your time spent on development. Your development officer(s) will always number fewer than needed, so you need to leverage department chairs and faculty to assist in the college's development efforts. Do so by ensuring all departments are receiving some attention from development, even if they seem to have poor prospects. When all departments are seeing some attention to their stated needs, they are much more likely to pass on referrals (good leads to potential donors) to your development staff and to help connect you with those individuals.

> *(BSD)* I have arranged with my development officer (as well as with their supervisor in the University Foundation) that a priority for the college is to have at least one individual in each department, each year being developed towards a major gift. Departments which had never sent a referral to the development officer are now doing so on almost a monthly basis, many of which are excellent prospects.

You should decide what communications with the college's previous and potential donors are personalized. From our experience in talking to donors, neither form letters nor letters containing general boilerplate text are engaging or satisfying for their recipients.

> *(BSD)* To this end, I set a threshold whereby gifts of $5,000 or more will receive a personalized letter from me (this has me writing 10-15 letters a month which is a reasonable load for me; you can set a threshold appropriate for your college). When I receive a gift, I have a system in place for a support staff member to send me the address and a few "facts" about the individual from their Foundation profile. I hand write a 5-6 sentence "thank you" card which incorporates some of those facts. I have learned many of these recipients keep my cards, and that they do not keep any of the other thank-you letters from the institution.
>
> *(JCH)* Some communications look more personal than they actually are. I have a special email account that shows my name, but is managed by the development staff. It is primarily used for communicating with my college's campaign committee. If someone responds to that account, the staff forwards the message to me and I respond from my personal email account.

As dean, you are accountable not only for the college's development strategy, but also for the success of your development officer. You can help organize your schedule and activities to help make him or her successful. The officer's success directly supports your college, and a good partnership will help you retain a good officer. Reserve several days for travel each semester and provide those dates to your development officer, but do not be surprised if appointments are possible for only a few of those dates. Many of your donors have schedules just as complicated as yours, so you will need to be flexible with your calendaring. Few on-campus meetings are critical; ask if you can be represented by an associate dean or department chair so that you can accommodate a visit with a potential donor. It will also be helpful to your development staff if you provide your conference/travel calendar at least a semester in advance so they can schedule appointments for you before, after or in time windows during your conference (e.g. now you have another reason to attend CCAS meetings!).

You are the chief academic officer for the college, which means your development officer will rely on you to communicate (in lay terms) the academic vision of the college and its programs to potential donors. Know your elevator speech for the college and for each of the major initiatives underway in the college. Regardless of where communications/marketing staff are housed, you are responsible for communication about the college. This includes your college and department websites, case statements for the college and major initiatives, press releases, as well as internal communication to your departments regarding development initiatives and successes. Ideally, the communications staff will align newsletters, articles, and web-materials with the development priorities for the college; donors will see this as a consistent message coming from the college.

> *(JCH)* When my development officer and I visit donors, we always bring a packet of materials to leave behind. For a first visit, this would normally include a selection of materials from the college and the department(s) representing the donor's affiliations or interests, as well as materials from the University capital campaign. The development officer and college communications director work together and with department chairs, so that we have an attractive brochure or "one-pager" for each department and research center in the college, providing quick facts, notable accomplishments of faculty and students, and a selection of giving opportunities. Depending on the donor, faculty publications—especially from history and creative writing—literary journals, and recordings, make meaningful gifts.

If your office is hiring a development officer (or if your institution is hiring one for you), make sure that you are heavily involved in the interview process. While Foundation staff or other development officers might be in the best position to judge an applicant's development skills, your personality must be a match with the individual who is hired. You will be travelling with this person frequently and must work closely together when making significant asks of donors. If a candidate is selected for you—even one with an excellent development pedigree—and their personality clashes with yours, the fundraising efforts of your college will suffer. Even if you do not know much about development, it is in your best interest to guide the selection process. If the development officer reports to the central Development Office (with "dotted line" to the dean), you may have little say about the position's title, but it can be helpful to include the phrase "alumni relations." One occasionally encounters alumni prospects that are skittish about speaking with someone from "development," but pleased by outreach from "alumni relations."

Development Officer

Whether you share a single development officer with other colleges or have multiple officers, development officers have common responsibilities. The development officer must know the technical side of giving (e.g., giving options, tax implications, what type of *quid pro quo* arrangements to avoid) and should possess the skills and knowledge necessary for developing donors (e.g., use of moves management, best phrasing to use when asking for visits and gifts, knowing when a potential donor is ready for an ask). The officer should readily adapt to your priorities in development for the college, and will quickly learn how best to support you for your development success.

Your development officer is responsible for constructing and then maintaining a portfolio of about 150 individuals in different stages of development. These stages tend to include identification (research has identified the individual as a prospect), discovery (an initial visit to determine if an individual may be philanthropically minded), cultivation (building the relationship of the donor to the institution), solicitation (a request for their financial support), and stewardship (showing the institution's appreciation of their gift). The officer will place individuals into a moves management system showing the date and outcome of last visit along with the estimated date of the next proposed activity with the individual. Keeping the portfolio filled and moving is a key responsibility; if some prospects are unresponsive or uninterested, the portfolio should be updated with new prospects. Using moves management, your development officer will be able to let you know when to write, call, or visit with donors, or other activities to move donors towards deeper engagement with the college.

The dean will rely on the development officer to prepare for visits with donors. The officer will provide you with information about the individual with whom you will be meeting, including notes from previous meetings (which you should read and remember for the visit). The briefing will include a walk-through of the expected flow of the meeting and suggest when to introduce specific topics; if it helps with mental preparation or nerves, an officer should be willing to role-play the meeting with you. Sometimes there are taboo subjects with donors (e.g. ex-spouse) and your development officer should inform you accordingly. Your development officer will assist in preparing case statements and letters of commitment, and as needed bring these along with other literature (e.g., news releases, building plans). If a gift is appropriate (often something bearing your institution's logo) the officer will bring it for the visit.

You might not feel ready to meet a donor—but that is why development officer comes along. The officer is there to improve your chance of success; to cover for you if you forget to introduce a topic at a specific time, forget someone's name, etc. It is best if the dean asks for the gift, but if you are uncomfortable asking for gifts, your development officer can do it. As the meeting draws to a close, the development officer will ensure that each participant knows the next steps. Afterwards, the development officer will either write directly to the prospect to say thank-you for the meeting, or prepare a letter to be sent from you, or both. The officer is responsible for writing notes about the visit and its outcome, the next step with the prospect, entering these into a database, and updating the move management system. Much time can pass between meetings; you and the development officer will meet many other people and without notes you will forget key information acquired during your meeting. If notice and have time windows to meet with individuals not in the development officer's main portfolio. If provided by your development officer, the assistant can keep track of the dean's action-items (e.g. have thank you letters for visits or gifts been written?); this keeps your development officer from spending time checking up on his or her over-committed and often-forgetful dean.

An administrative assistant hired by the Foundation will have a job description much more focused towards development activities. Foundation-funded assistants will be involved with more prospect research, will help or even lead on event planning involving donors, and maintain communication with members of external college boards. In the absence of such an assistant from the Foundation, event planning and communication with the board will need to be delegated, to either your administrative assistant (which could involve a change in job description) or additional clerical staff in your office. Do not let your development officer become bogged down with clerical tasks.

Conversely, an administrative assistant should never take on a role suited for a development officer, such as making cold calls to set up appointments for the officer or for you. Your administrative assistant has not been trained to be effective in this role, and is unlikely to enjoy it. The assistant's morale suffers, as does the chance of securing a successful visit.

> *(BSD)* I asked a former development officer to set up a cold call dinner with four or five alumni when I would have a free evening at a conference. Despite several months of advanced notice, no dinner materialized. The problem? While we had a long-list of very successful alums in the city, the development officer had assigned the cold call responsibilities to the administrative assistant. While the assistant honestly (and repeatedly) tried, no one would commit to dinner. Would you react any differently to such a phone call or letter?

Department Chairs and Assistant/Associate Deans

Alumni engagement and referrals are the top two functions for the college's other administrative members. As pointed out in earlier chapters, Arts and Sciences graduates will generally associate with their departments, not the college. Therefore, they are most likely to attend events, read newsletters, or respond to requests from the heads of departments rather than from the dean. Events like theatre and orchestral performances also attract individuals from the community and alumni from other colleges who may be interested in supporting the arts. Each department often has an "alumnus of the year" which recruits these individuals back to campus for a recognition ceremony. The more activities open to alumni and the community that the department sponsors, the more likely they will generate referrals.

Referrals are the names of individuals that department chairs and assistant/associate deans send to your development officer to learn whether they may be major gift prospects or at least annual giving prospects. Referrals may come about when an alumnus sends updated information to a department, but they occur more often when alumni attend events and appear interested in one or more initiatives underway in the department. When a referral is sent, additional information (if known) should be sent to your officer including degree program, year of graduation, current employer, and any other information of interest (e.g. their business is taking off, etc.). The development officer (or administrative assistant) will check the database for additional information on the individual. If the information from the referral or from the database looks promising, these referrals will become part of the development officer's portfolio. A prospect who has already demonstrated engagement with the department is more promising than a random draw from the database. Departments that send referrals will end up with more major gift prospects being developed, which encourages them to buy into the referral process and support it with further referrals. When sufficient referrals are being submitted from your departments, you have a strong case for adding development staff to your college.

The very ease with which departments connect to alumni raises the nettlesome issue of maintaining accurate addresses for the college's alumni. Your institution has a centralized database where all alumni addresses are kept. Departments are frustrated with this database, as they are frequently restricted from full access to this information (due to efforts of the institution to coordinate mailings, including annual giving requests), or they find the addresses out of date. The tactic your departments will employ is to build a 'ghost' database which they maintain and update, but they don't share their information with the central database. Your departments do not need to waste their time keeping such databases: some alumni send address updates elsewhere in the institution; thus, a department's database will also become inaccurate. In return for not keeping a 'ghost' database, the University must provide unfettered access to the addresses of each department's alumni, and the department must agree to coordinate mass-mailings with the institution. Departments within Arts and Sciences contact vast numbers of alumni for outreach and annual giving, so this is a reasonable compromise which is best for the institution as a whole.

Department chairs will often know more than the dean about initiatives in departments or centers, and they may enthusiastically be able to represent them. Some priorities for funding will be straight forward for you to explain (e.g. adding freshman scholarships), while others will be complex and more often than not out of your area of expertise (e.g. adding a research center). So ask your chairs and assistant/associate deans for help in developing prospects for complex projects. Remember, you want to raise funds for the college. It does not matter who helps the potential donor to see the value in a project. The donor must be connected to the project and the institution, not just to you. Also, by getting your chairs involved in development, they will better appreciate the process and the time that you invest in it.

If you get department chairs or your associate deans involved in a development project and they are to meet with the potential donors, they must be coached on what to do and when to do it at the meeting. Either you take on this responsibility for coaching, or delegate it to your development officer. When they are prepared for a meeting in the same way as your development officer prepares you, your department chairs can be very effective in asking for major gifts.

(BSD) In one visit, involving two donors, me, a University Development officer, and a center director, we had just sat down to present a "major ask" when the center director unrolled a building plan on

the table, and proceeded to explain the plan to one of the donors who seemed excited about the project. The other donor received little of the director's attention during this presentation, and alienated, ended up not supporting the plan. And it was my fault—I did not explain in advance the timing of the meeting and how this center director's plans would be incorporated.

> *(JCH)* Not all chairs are at ease with the ask, yet their role is crucial in leading up to that stage. A strategy that has worked well for one department with a large alumni base in a major metropolitan area two hours from our campus: working with my office, the department organizes a faculty panel around a timely topic of general interest, to be held in a convenient downtown location. An hour-long reception follows the panel. Following the reception, the chair and I host an intimate dinner for a few major prospects, at which we come to know them better and, depending on the group and the moment, make an elevator pitch for a particular initiative.

Improving the Performance of the Dean's Office

Management books profess that establishing trust is a key, if not the key, component in working relationships. Development officers are expected be the best at solicitation strategies; understanding college politics and leading faculty are not part of their skill set. Deans have been selected by their colleagues because they are the best managers and leaders for the college's academic improvement; fundraising is not our primary responsibility. Therefore mutual trust is a prerequisite for this relationship; you must trust that your development officer is the best placed individual to provide *you* with feedback on how you can improve in your development role for the college. As part of trust, being able to accept candid and constructive feedback from each other is critical for improving the development capabilities of the office.

As a dean, you are familiar with an annual review process which includes a summative appraisal and formative development meeting. While such an annual review is important, it is not the most important type of feedback for improving development visits. We recommend that you and your development officer discuss what went well and what could be improved *immediately* after the visit concludes. Only then will you be able to discuss wording, timing, the donor's reaction, etc. Making this conversation a compulsory part of your visit routine will quickly make it feel normal for both of you. You both must be explicit about who should change what at the next visit, which means you (even as dean) should accept, and thank, constructive criticism.

> *(BSD)* After one visit concluded with a prospect who said "just ask if you need anything," my development officer reminded me that would have been an ideal time to make a "soft ask," where I would have set up an appointment to discuss with them funding for a specific initiative in the college. I thanked my officer for the feedback, and encouraged her to provide more in the future.

> *(JCH)* In my early months as dean, my development officer was already in the final stages of planning two major events in two distant cities. I was too inexperienced at the time to see—although realization dawned very soon—that the development officer had taken on far too many practical and logistical tasks, to the detriment of any significant cultivation of donor relationships. The events were "successful" to the extent that they went well and were enjoyed by those who were present, but both represented huge investments of time and resources with little, if any, tangible results. Lesson learned! The officer left not long thereafter. My current officer and I are much more judicious in the investment of each other's time.

As noted in Chapter 1, the development officer and support staff may report directly or indirectly to a central Development Office. Regardless of who carries out the formal personnel review, you will want to have a good working relationship with the development officer's "other" supervisor. If either side perceives problems in the development officer's performance, this should be discussed and feedback coordinated. If the officer is employed by a central office, then it should provide you with performance statistics (numbers of visits, proposals, and solicitations) and progress toward annual goals on a regular basis. Being further from the action, the central office will almost inevitably view performance in terms of those statistics and the college development officer may feel pressured to move relationships along more quickly than "feels" right. Your own judgment is important here, as is frank and open communication with the central office.

Professional development and continuing education are critical to all of us, especially we who have spent most of our careers as faculty and department chairs. If the University organizes workshops and talks by outside consultants from the development world, take advantage of them and encourage your staff and department chairs to do so as well. Take part in sessions on fundraising at conferences such as CCAS. Encourage mutual mentoring among your staff and between them and their counterparts in other parts of the University.

Collaborations within the College and across Campus

As noted in Chapter 2, alumni affinities and philanthropic interests can extend well beyond their "home" department, and some alumni will have more than one home if they double-majored, or completed an undergraduate degree in Arts and Sciences and a graduate degree in one of the professional schools, if their spouse is affiliated with a different campus unit, or if their cultural and philanthropic interests have broadened to areas beyond their own studies and profession. Successful women, for example, may choose to support a Women's Studies Department that did not exist when they were students. Managing the network of relationships and interests requires tact, not only with the prospects, but also with one's fellow deans. Ground rules must be established as to who has the primary relationship, but all deans must be willing to "share" and accept that prospects may have multiple interests and multiple loyalties.

Many campus development offices have traditionally directed outreach and development efforts to the male of alumni couples, ignoring the woman's affiliations. Fortunately, times have changed. Depending on the couple's wishes, the central Development Office may be helpful in choreographing a dance that involves both members of a couple, two deans, and two college development officers. In such an instance, it will take time and delicate negotiation to create a major gift proposal, but the donors appreciate the coordination and the respect shown to the totality of their interests.

> *(JCH)* The other dean and I have coordinated our efforts, often with central development to facilitate the conversations. When one such couple (he, a real estate developer and she, a writer, both from modest backgrounds) made it clear that they shared a common passion for helping others rise above economic hardship, we crafted a joint proposal that includes funding for major scholarship and outreach initiatives in both colleges.

Similar situations arise within the college. Department chairs must be prepared for the possibility that a relationship that they have brought forward and cultivated may ultimately be to another's benefit. One cannot say too often that it is all to the good of the college and the University. One way of mitigating such disappointments is to offer donors a full spectrum of department-level and college-level opportunities. A college-level scholarship fund and a fund for visiting scholars and artists, for example, benefit all departments. Creating a culture of development throughout the college will inform and sensitize department chairs and faculty members to the realities and nuances of fundraising.

Working with the development officer, departments should be encouraged to take advantage of noteworthy events and anniversaries to bring attention to their activities and energize their supporters and alums. Your officer can meet with the chair and key members of the department to discuss an action plan: enlisting a departmental advisory board, organizing a special event, cultivating key prospects. Emeritus faculty can often be among the most powerful advocates and promoters of the department, having (usually) greater time to devote to special projects and (often) a large cohort of alumni contacts.

Working with External Boards

Virtually all colleges and many academic departments have some form of advisory board composed of alumni and "friends." Advisory boards of any sort require an investment of time and attention; they may meet annually or sometimes more often, on campus or in a nearby city. Staff resources need to be deployed to maintain contact and meeting agendas must be carefully constructed. Board members wish to be useful and feel engaged; an agenda composed primarily of news items and "talking heads" will not be as effective as one that calls on members' expertise and that capitalizes on the opportunity for discussion. A board meeting held on campus presents an excellent opportunity for members to meet students, perhaps over dinner or in a career networking event. The opportunity to meet with students, to offer advice, to hear about their goals and dreams, to appreciate their accomplishments, is an extraordinarily powerful form of engagement for board members.

> *(BSD)* At my former institution, which had a limited history of philanthropy, the chair of the advisory board and I agreed to introduce a commitment to giving for new and reappointed board members. During their three year terms, board members would be expected to give $25,000 (cash or cash equivalent) or greater to the college personally, through their companies, or through individuals that they networked to the college. This resulted in a few endowments, but also gifts of major equipment, sponsored research, and internships. Over a five-year period and asking more than a dozen new individuals to join the board, only one individual declined to join the board due to this giving request.

Not all advisory boards are formed with an eye toward fundraising, but given the time required to make a board meeting successful and the increased importance of development in the life of the college, some blending of the two should be considered. Every college has deeply committed alumni who have much to offer students, but who lack the financial capacity to make major gifts. You could find other roles for them: for example reading internal scholarship applications, participating in a career night, or helping to organize an event in another city.

A campaign committee is a much more focused entity and in many ways much easier to manage, as its mission is clear—as is the expectation of a financial contribution. Once a critical mass is attained, size matters less than dedication and willingness to commit one's time and resources. While balanced representation from the college disciplines is desirable, breadth and diversity of interests and career paths are more important. The committee's chairs or co-chairs work closely with the college development officer to finish recruiting the committee and to establish each member's role. Part of the recruiting process involves educating members about the nature and stages of development work.

> *(JCH)* It was a meeting of this sort that gave our campaign committee its first experience of making cold calls. Following the committee meeting, which took place at a downtown University club, we held a larger "Meet-the-Dean" reception for a wider circle of alumni. Each committee member had contacted 10–15 other alums in the area to invite them to the reception. The committee discovered that making the calls was more enjoyable than they had expected.

It is reassuring to many to understand that, unless they are experienced and comfortable with that role, they need not be involved in making an ask. More often, they are requested to develop networks of other alumni or professional peers; to invite others to campaign events; to host events themselves. They also lead by example. At an event celebrating a particular initiative or project, for example, the testimony of a campaign committee member who stands and asks others to join in support can be highly effective in motivating others.

> *(JCH)* I inherited an advisory board that had largely lost its sense of purpose; only a small core continued to come to the campus for meetings and they were not accustomed to any expectations of annual giving. The start of a University

> capital campaign provided an opportunity to renew the board. Active advisory board members of appropriate means were invited to join the campaign committee, which carried the expectation of a major gift. Active members of the advisory board who lacked major financial means have eagerly accepted other roles. I wrote a friendly letter to each inactive member, suggesting various forms of engagement, but also offering a face-saving "way out," since the formal advisory board was to be suspended for the duration of the capital campaign. A few were clearly grateful for the opportunity to resign gracefully; they remain friends of the college and part of our extended network.

The campaign committee's time is a precious resource. Multiple meetings will be needed in the early stages of a major campaign; each should have a clear objective and purpose. The committee can preview campaign materials and help the dean and development officer refine their messaging; they can help one another conceptualize and develop special projects; they can learn more about the college. At an early point in the campaign, particularly if some committee members are still contemplating their leadership gifts, an extended session with the campus's planned giving officer may be enlightening. Even alumni who work in the financial sector may not be aware of all the intricacies of charitable gift annuities. Committee members find such information useful for themselves and it also becomes part of their repertory in conversations with others.

Bringing the committee to campus offers the opportunity to meet faculty and students engaged in particular projects: for example, a summer archaeology institute, or a digital humanities initiative, or a science camp for pre-college students. Such encounters fire the imagination, make the alumni proud of their institution, provide them with concrete details to describe to others, and renew their enthusiasm and commitment.

If the campus is not in an urban center, it may be practical to hold at least some of the meetings in a city with a major transportation hub.

Such a meeting can be combined with additional outreach and cultivation activities.

> *(BSD)* At my former institution, the college's advisory board agreed to host one meeting per year at a board member's business. Over a three-year period, we met (and received comprehensive tours) at a major logistics center, a green chemical company, and one of the nation's largest food producers. All the companies employed alumni from the college, so the board members experienced the diversity of the careers entered by our graduates, and they had a "stimulating" tour of business with which they were not familiar. Outside of hearing from students, many board members indicated this was the highlight of being on the board (which helped in recruiting new members).

Starting from Nothing

If your college does not have a development officer or a budget earmarked for development, you may wonder how to get started. If you are questioning if development is even worth the effort, think about your own financial planning: you have been saving money towards a financially secure retirement—does your college deserve any less? Development provides your college with financial security for the future.

If no resources are provided to your college for development, creating a position for a development officer out of the college's budget may be unsustainable. You must make the case for at least a shared officer for the college, either to the institution's Development Office (more likely) or to academic affairs (less likely). The institution will want assurance of a high return-on-investment (ROI); meaning if they provide the salary for an officer, this individual has a high-likelihood of securing many times their salary in gifts back to the college. In making the case for a high ROI, you will need to invest your time into development to show you are ready for this responsibility. Reading this book should not be the end of your professional development in fundraising: at least attend a development conference (e.g. CASE's "Development for Deans" workshop). You can start an advisory board for the college with a giving requirement. Construct a list of referrals from your department chairs and faculty comprised of individuals highly engaged with the departments and students; update and forward this list to the development office/academic affairs regularly. Through your leadership, you can demonstrate that the college has engaged alumni that provide gifts to the college, warranting at least a shared development officer. Even if your college does not receive a development officer in the near-term, you are organizing the college to follow high-impact practices for development which will nonetheless help the long-term financial health of your college.

Conclusion

When you first look at development operations in your office, you may feel as if you want to grab the nearest broom, sweep out the existing practices and build everything from scratch. That might work. Yet staff, just like faculty, can be surprisingly resistant to change—trying to implement too much change too quickly may lead to disaster. In Chapter 2, Moen suggests that your first step in development should start with the existing structure; we agree. As you familiarize yourself with that structure and match existing responsibilities to the expected norms for the positions, talk to your staff about pros and cons of possible changes and then progressively implement the changes that are the most likely to be effective for you and your institution.

You will never have enough development officers to reach all of your alumni, so the assistance of your department chairs and associate deans is important, particularly in Arts and Sciences, where prospective donors often identify with their former departments. Once your chairs become involved in development, steer them away from the idea that every referral they provide will result in a gift back to their department. John F. Kennedy often said that "A rising tide lifts all boats," a phrase that well represents the desirable team mentality of development: you cannot predict where gifts will end up, so any outcome that lands a gift anywhere in the college—or even elsewhere in the institution is still a positive outcome.

Your development officer is the key to realizing the fundraising goals that you set for your college. You are quite likely to spend more time with your development officer than any other individual at the University: on the phone, in meetings, and on the road. Carefully choose a personality and skill set that complements your strengths and mitigates your weaknesses in working with donors. Once you are working together, you need to support each other by candidly discussing what is working in your partnership and what can be improved. Through this maturing partnership, you will find that the development of donors provides a refreshing pause from your other decanal responsibilities.

It is probably safe to say that none of us became professors and later deans because we were interested in fundraising; indeed, the very word often makes faculty members wince. In our experience, however, development is often one of the most enjoyable parts of the job. It offers opportunities to meet people from many walks of life, to learn what their education has meant to their lives, and to spread the word about the good work being done by faculty and students. Meeting alumni will also provide you with ever-new answers to parents' eternal question, "What can my child do with a major in X?" Through practice, you will become accomplished in telling your institution's story, and in advocating for the liberal arts.

4

Finding Money and Raising Funds

D.J. Trela, Richard Finkelstein and Lori Vermeulen

Finding and raising money is akin to gardening or gathering a harvest. Friend and fundraising is both art and science and may look easy, but takes more work and time than one might expect. It isn't just a matter of picking the apples off the tree in September, or cutting roses for a centerpiece in June. You have to consider all the stages that get you to the point of harvest and how each of those stages contributes to its abundance. In farming, you clear the land, enrich the soil, choose plants suited to your planting zone, fertilize, and prune. The proper tending of the garden precedes any harvest and directly affects its quality. You also need to harvest at the right time and in the right way. Anyone can stick a flower in the ground or plant a tree and hope it will grow. But optimal results take time, care and attention.

This metaphor works in the world of development. Donors need to be identified just as do proper plants. We use a farming term to talk about work with potential and actual donors in that they need to be "cultivated." In the fundraising world, cultivation involves the work of identifying likely donors, their interests, passions and desired levels of engagement. When we talk about securing a gift from donors, we speak in terms of an ask, but the positive result in the form of a gift is similar to the harvest. Properly done, fundraising offers a high probability of success, because we have done everything needed to cultivate the donor. In fundraising we use the term stewardship to refer to how gifts are received and how donors are managed. The gift itself needs to be used for its intended purpose. The donors need to be reminded regularly of the

> as the older and wealthier donor base passed away, no new donors replaced them. As an institution, it nearly needed to start over to build the infrastructure the previous vice-chancellor had neglected.

Knowing where your institution stands in terms of engagement with alumni and donors is essential before plunging into the fundraising realm yourself. The stages of donor development are relatively easily defined. The hard work comes in building and sustaining an infrastructure that supports and encourages giving at all levels.

Regardless of your institution's history and level of engagement, you generally can rely on at least partial partnership with an Advancement Office, or, better yet, a designated development officer. Depending on local circumstances, you may be able to direct resources to the hire of a development officer under your direction, or have a dotted line relationship with an advancement officer who may also be working with other deans, chairs, or executive officers. Having an effective, highly functioning development officer is one of the smartest long-term investments you can make, and it is also among the most difficult to secure. The critical resources of time, money and personnel are always limited, but, at the least, you need an assistant to facilitate and set up meetings with actual and potential donors, formulate asks, develop proposals, and engage in stewardship activities for your active donors. Keep in mind that a key aspect of a successful partnership is that you and your development officer complement each other's strengths and weaknesses. Knowing your own weaknesses and communicating them clearly to your gift officer will make for a more enjoyable and successful fund-raising experience. (This chapter's lead author is somewhat phone-phobic, but can write excellent thank-you letters, is a good public speaker, and interacts effectively in small groups. His major gift officer was excellent on the phone, an insightful listener, and an excellent researcher. They both shared a passion for the college and University on whose behalf they advocated. Complementary strengths made them a better team.)

Fundraising is but part of a larger portfolio of duties, and it is often viewed by your faculty colleagues as more critical to your role as dean than apparent "hobnobbing with friends" and "going to parties." To preserve your sanity and make progress on fundraising, you need a good development officer who will work with you to most effectively utilize your strengths and your valuable time.

Do you have a Communications Strategy that Brings your College into the Lives of Alumni and Other Supporters on a Regular Basis?

An alumni relations office that communicates regularly with graduates, maintains accurate addresses, and provides opportunities for alumni to return to campus for special events is a key part of the infrastructure that needs to be in place to support your efforts. Scheduled, meaningful contact with your graduates (and other institutional friends) is fundamental. Absent the required infrastructure, some first steps might include consulting with departments that have contact with some of their former students. Some may put out newsletters or routinely update department websites with news of graduates. Theatre and Music Departments normally have events to which the public is invited, and so will have valid address lists. Biology or Chemistry departments like to keep track of their pre-med or pre-dental graduates who have gone on to graduate or professional school. And individual faculty members often stay in contact with former students for years and decades after their graduation. These departments and individuals are sources of information that can help you build a base of friends and donors for your college, particularly if centralized resources are limited or non-existent. Many of these departments may themselves have raised modest funds over the years and their chairs may be willing to share with you the names of loyal supporters, especially if you can explain that you can assist in the fundraising process and potential gifts will not be diverted to you.

If you have a robust alumni relations operation on your campus, express an eagerness to work more closely with its staff. You likely will be greeted with enthusiasm, since these are not areas where deans have often been active. Work to draw in larger departments, and chairs or faculty, who are good spokespersons. Use alumni relations staff to devise events that can showcase your college, improve communications with alumni, and routinely update them. A robust alumni relations operation is a vital step in friendraising, and friends are more likely to donate to your cause than strangers. Keeping in touch with your alumni maintains bonds of loyalty they may feel to their University, college, school, major department, or even to individual faculty who supported them when they were undergraduates.

If your development operation or that of your University is relatively new, an effective communications strategy between you and your potential supporters is critically important; it should probably precede plans to raise significant amounts of money or to identify needs and solicit gifts for them. Most institutions publish alumni magazines on a quarterly or semi-annual basis. The trend is towards more online forms of communication, particularly with younger alumni. You should work with the communications team, which is often part of the Advancement area, to inform them of needs you have defined for your college so they can create related articles trumpeting the accomplishments of your faculty and more successful alumni.

Whether or not you can work closely with Communications staff, you should communicate regularly with your alumni to create new connections and prospects. Your instruments need not be elaborate or especially sophisticated: your main goal is to make your college a presence in the lives of your constituents. Alumni and supporters are often more interested in current students and other alumni than they are in faculty or their publications. A newsletter should also include an invitation to contact you individually to tell you about themselves or their experience of the college. Including a form for donations (and a statement that they be designated for your college) may not yield you many direct returns but reminds them about giving opportunities and that they can direct later gifts to your area.

Even in this Internet era, you may have success with semi-annual newsletters of four to six pages that include a letter from the dean speaking in a very positive tone about recent exciting activities or successes in the college; one or two features about students who have an interesting story or accomplishment that can be told; and similar stories about faculty known to be popular.

A simple but effective action you can take in building or reinforcing connections with your supporters is to put a personal note on such communications before they are mailed. We recommend this touch after you research prior contributions over a threshold you have identified, or for people you want to cultivate. The note can be extremely brief: e.g. "Thanks for your support—please let me know what you are doing." In an era of mail-merged, form-letter responses, a personal note of thanks appended to a letter can be a powerful acknowledgement.

If you have the technological support, print newsletters should be supplemented with electronic communications. E-mail updates to constituents about events and ongoing activities are still important. Because frequency of communications is the real issue, we invite alumni and supporters to events even though we know that people are unlikely to travel distances to attend them. As with invitations, Facebook pages further your goal of helping your constituents feel they remain part of the college family. The use of Twitter additionally moves that goal forward. The guiding principles behind these communications are staying in people's lives so they feel good about being connected to your college and its successes. What you say is less important than communicating frequently.

How do you Identify New Donors and Gradually Expand the Pool of Donors?

Consider the different groups of individuals who, for different reasons, may want to support a College or University. In our experience the primary categories, in relative order of importance, are:

Former students or graduates who are deeply grateful for the education they received, with an impulse to "give back." Very often they are first generation graduates, or students whose education was made possible by scholarships, or students whose lives were irrevocably and positively touched by particular faculty or staff. This group also includes legacy families proud of a multi-generational relationship with your University, one which should be specially cultivated in communications, publications, and direct outreach. These natural donors will be enormously valuable to an institution when properly cultivated. (At one of our institutions, the largest donor to the University speaks eloquently about how scholarships made his education–and that of many of his twelve siblings–possible. He also speaks about how as he was being admitted to the University, its chancellor told him scholarships were making his education possible and that once he graduated, he had an obligation to "give back.") One of your tasks is to identify these grateful graduates and convince them to increase their own giving to the institution that enabled their success. So how do you identify them? There's no sure-fire method, but here are some things to keep in mind:

- Aside from receiving the regular newsletter, have they been connected to your institution recently? Consider hosting an interesting event that casts a wide net. New donors can be identified when they accept an invitation to participate in a University event that will re-connect them to their alma mater. For example, host a family planetarium show for alumni who live in the area. Target the invitation to those who are likely to have school-age children and make it a family event. Or, host a networking event for women in science that will showcase current accomplishments of female faculty and students. Invite your alumni who are women in science and ask for their assistance as mentors.

- Are they already giving, and to what? Current support means something. If a recent graduate has established a pattern of giving, this is likely to continue throughout his or her life. Look at the records, observe the patterns, and decide which donors to investigate and cultivate further. Consider hosting events thanking donors for their previous contributions to a particular department, program, or cause.

- Are they volunteers for your college or the University? Do they return to events after their graduation? It's possible they might not have the means of making a donation, but if they are demonstrating institutional loyalty, this can eventually be translated into a financial commitment.

Faculty and staff who have spent the bulk of their careers at your institution. Consider hosting an annual event for retired faculty and staff. Invite them to a local garden or museum for a private tour as a way of thanking them for their service to the institution. Use the opportunity to update them on the activities of the college. They may see themselves as individuals whose lives have been enriched by their association with your institution but have no immediate family or dependents with a claim on their resources or estate.

> At one of our institutions a long-time secretary, who had never married, made an estate plan that resulted in more than a $600,000 endowment that provided support to fund undergraduate students presenting their research at academic conferences or engaged in some form of undergraduate research. In other instances, three faculty members made estate gifts that supported the Physics program, the History program, and, more generally, research in the humanities. Combined, these gifts totaled over $8 million.

Loyal faculty and staff are among the most under-cultivated major donors to a college or University. Along with school teachers, they often don't see themselves as wealthy and may be especially responsive to careful cultivation and stewardship.

Local foundations, businesses or civic-minded individuals may not be alumni, but recognize the value a College or University brings to a community. There may be community-based foundations or corporations that see the importance of supporting local institutions of higher education. It is quite common for prominent local businesses to sponsor cultural or educational activities that help showcase their products and civic-mindedness. Although gifts of this sort are not completely altruistic, they can be a way of gaining modest and needed annual support for a vital college activity. This is all the more likely if 1) the business has a history of philanthropy, and 2) the business employs some of your graduates who might be in a position to influence the charitable giving of the organization.

> A case in point involved a prominent family who had influence over charitable giving that exceeded what they themselves could personally contribute. A member of this family had left the city of his birth, but never forgotten it. The bulk of his estate accrued to a foundation established upon his death. A family member who remained in the city where he was born sat on the foundation board. By working with the board member and her family, a proposal for an endowed research fund of $500,000 was put forward and approved. After the five years it took to establish this initial endowment, regular stewardship had built a strong relationship with the family and we were in a position to ask for a larger gift to support an instrumentation endowment. Because the family valued the presence of the University in the community and perceived that their initial gift had been well-stewarded, the second and larger ask was a comparatively easy one to make.

Parents of current students are more involved in their children's higher education experience than ever before. The Development Office is likely to be tracking people with considerable means who are non-alumni parents of current students. They may even have a council of current parents along with a parental fund-raising annual campaign. If your institution has this program, ask for opportunities to interact with this group so that they can hear about your vision and about the activities in your college. Both you and the development team will benefit. Another way to identify appreciative parents of your current students is to invite them to award ceremonies that honor their children.

How do you Cultivate Individuals that have Given as well as Those Who have Not?

Finding new donors and moving existing donors along a continuum of giving will keep your fundraising activities in healthy balance. Fundraising activities on this continuum give donors opportunities to increase the amounts. Each is vitally important, since the more elemental levels should be viewed as stepping stones to major gifts, or even transformational gifts. These areas include:

- ANNUAL GIVING OR ANNUAL APPEALS–relatively broad appeals for gifts ideally unrestricted in nature that can be expended on any project deemed worthwhile or necessary. New donors can pop up in the routine annual appeals. At one institution, seemingly out of the blue, an alumnus made a first gift of $1,000 in response to an annual appeal. Follow-up by the major gifts officer and the dean led to annual gifts of $25,000 in unrestricted funds from this donor within a year of receiving the first gift. It's important to realize that this is far from the norm, but without an annual appeal, neither the first $1,000 nor the much larger $25,000 gifts would have been made.

- MAJOR GIFTS–depending on your institution, these dollar amounts will vary from minimums of $5,000 on the lower end, to $100,000 at the higher end. If your institution does not have a robust history of significant giving from donors, your initial definition of "major" will be at the lower end of the spectrum. Moving a donor from providing a semi-regular annual gift to a major gift represents a significant step. A first gift is rarely a major gift, so the stepping stone of the Annual Appeal is critical.

- PLANNED GIVING–This category overlaps with major gifts and bequests. Prior to soliciting planned gifts, your institution should have policies and procedures in place that have been reviewed by your institution's lawyer or a trusts and estates attorney. Donors considering a planned gift also should be encouraged to consult with their attorneys or accountant. Among many reasons for reviewing your procedures with lawyers is that federal tax rules governing such gifts change. Planned gifts include Charitable Remainder Trusts, bequests made in a will (see below), annuities, or other legal instruments. Depending upon the instrument they choose, donors, and possibly their offspring, may maintain varying levels of control over the money throughout their lifetime. Although the benefits to your institution are obvious, there may also be considerable benefits to donors, including tax savings for them and their estate, and enhanced income from annuities they may receive. Your University can usually make such annuities available at a rate higher than commercially marketed instruments, at the same time providing them with a tax deduction for the gift that created the income.

- BEQUESTS–Often individuals want to remember their alma mater in their estate plan. Sometimes they assign a percentage of their estate to your institution and sometimes a fixed dollar amount or a particular asset, such as real estate. Because a will can be changed at any time, donors may change their minds without informing the legatee. It is thus crucial to exercise especially attentive stewardship for supporters who have chosen these means for giving.

- CAPITAL CAMPAIGN–This involves a longer period of more robust fundraising where institutions set larger dollar goals for fundraising over a multi-year period. Campaigns can range from relatively modest dollar amounts, as low as several million dollars for institutions with little to no history of raising funds, to multi-billion dollar campaigns operated by the most elite private and flagship state Universities. Campaigns are divided into steps that include planning and "silent" phases before the formal, public launch. During the more public phase, gifts are pursued with greater fanfare. Annual giving amounts are almost always included in the totals for capital campaigns. While the goal of a Capital Campaign is to raise money, it also should increase the number of donors overall, as well as their giving levels so that, once the Campaign is over, the institution will be able to rely, annually, on a higher level of giving from a greater number of donors.

In developing donors, consider what motivates individuals to give. People want to support what they already perceive is successful, people like to be part of something that is larger or bigger than themselves, people are often motivated to "give back," and some people genuinely appreciate the fuss that is made about them when they are identified as significant donors to an institution. Most of us have more ego than we like to admit, although some donors prefer to remain anonymous.

Donors are passionate about the cause or institution. Listen carefully to your potential donors and match their true passions to your college's needs. Trying to convince people to have passion about one of your highest priorities when their highest priority lies somewhere else is *not* an effective strategy for raising friends or funds. You can insure that your college is on your donors' "A" list when you show respect for their passions and provide them with options that match them. People give because they are asked. Not asking is probably the biggest single mistake those of us engaged in fundraising can make. (One of the authors of this chapter supported his University with a modest annual gift of $500. When he left to take a position in another state, he would have continued these gifts given the good relationship he had with the University, but since he was never asked, he redirected his charitable giving elsewhere.)

- People like to give to an enterprise that is already successful. Understanding why your potential donor finds your institution successful or not successful is critical. Educating them about your successes and how their gift can make a difference will show that you understand and respect their definition of success. And when it comes to alumni, point to *them* as one of your institution's success stories!

- People like to give to an enterprise that has clear and rational plans for the future that are consistent with its mission, and a record of implementing its plans. Share with donors your strategic plan, or if bricks-and-mortar are you goal, a long-range facilities plan.

- Some individuals and businesses appreciate the value that a University brings to their town or region of the state. While they may not be alumni, they recognize the institution provides their businesses with employees, brings stature and status to the community, and enriches the intellectual, cultural and economic life of the community. They support an enterprise that contributes to the vitality of community—and to their own financial success.

- People increasingly give in support of specific projects or programs, rather than to undesignated purposes. (It's hard to be passionate about replacing an air conditioning system or boiler, but it can be enormously uplifting for a donor to meet a recipient of a scholarship they endowed.)

As an exercise, you might examine your own practice of giving. What do you support? Why? How much of your own income or savings do you contribute annually? What would it take for you to be willing to double the amount you give to your favorite charity on an annual basis? To set up an endowment during your lifetime? To include an organization in your estate plan? These are exactly the sorts of questions you will be asking of potential donors, both directly and indirectly. Your own motivations and rationales are not likely to differ from those of your actual and potential donors, and so can serve to guide you. If you do not have a habit of giving to the institution for which you are expected to raise money, you will have a harder time convincing others that they should provide support.

How do you know when to Ask? For what? For how much?

Making the ask includes 1) identifying the needs of your college, articulating them concisely in a case statement, and 2) matching these needs to the individuals who are most likely and ready to support those needs. This sounds straightforward, but the steps, stages, sub-stages and moves that might need to occur when working with a donor can be time-consuming or frustrating. But you will experience an exhilarating moment when a donor embraces a project with great enthusiasm. To identify and articulate unit needs, follow these steps:

- Consult broadly with your faculty, chairs, directors, and advisory board members to identify priorities. From this you should develop a long list of unit needs. When consulting with your faculty, you need to make it clear that: 1) you want their ideas, 2) you need their expertise in crafting proposals, but 3) you can't guarantee the results. A common misconception among faculty is that donors do indeed grow on trees, and that it is a simple matter of walking to the orchard at harvest time to gather scholarships or an endowed professorship for a grateful department. If you are working in a mature operation where donors are plentiful and have been cultivated for decades, that might occur. But this is far from the norm.

- Be clear about your own vision for your academic unit. The proposals from the faculty will provide you with a series of relatively specific needs that can be used to stimulate initial interest from a donor interested in making a gift. However, your donors are looking to you for leadership. Articulating your vision of how these items fit into the strategic directions that you have for your college will be important to the savvy donor.

Pay close attention to initiatives outlined in any strategic planning or master plan documents for your unit or campus. Prepare a case statement that in a few pages describes the program, scholarship, or physical plant project that you want to acquire, and gives a persuasive rationale for it in terms of the mission, goals, and potential for student success within the college. Show how your initiative fits into the University's master plan. Your University's Development staff should be eager and able to assist you with drafting the case statement. In a sense, the case statement is a sophisticated sales brochure for the project to which you hope someone will contribute. Potential donors will want to see such a document.

Once you have articulated your needs for your college, the search begins for the likely donors. Your Development Office can conduct research on their "capacity" or "capability." Various software programs

Think of this meeting as two people deciding on a future partnership; you want to persuade your counterpart of a good fit. You agree on a purpose. The donor has the money; you have the resources, the institution, expertise and people, to use it for your common goal. Be on time for the appointment. Be ready to provide a brief update on your college, identifying changes new to the alum. Be attentive to the alum's questions and interests. Encourage the alum to discuss his or her work and career and the part your college played. Take mental notes and record them as soon as possible after the meeting concludes. Be prepared to leave as soon as your time is up, but be willing to stay longer if the alum is interested in continuing the conversation. Wrap up the meeting with an invitation for further interaction, such as:

- Invite them to lecture at your campus or meet to with undergraduates in their discipline the next time they are in town.
- Find out when they will next be on your campus and invite them for a personal tour so they can see how it has grown and developed since their graduation.
- Depending on their enthusiasm and interest, ask them how they could see themselves more involved in the life of the college.
- Consider inviting them to sit on a relevant advisory board, if you have one to which they can meaningfully contribute.

When the visit ends, take the first opportunity to record important information garnered from the meeting. Provide it to your Development Office so that it can become part of a contact report, which includes the substance of the conversation, salient personal details, and the "next steps" alluded to above. A sample report could run something like the following:

> Dean Jones met with Mary Smith, a 1985 English graduate, for lunch on April 25, 2013. Smith became a partner in the nationally prominent law firm of Titus-Oates in 2005. She is divorced, with two college-aged daughters. During the meeting, I updated her on the new Masters in Writing program

> and the recent retirement of Professor Johnson. Smith asked about students going to law school and expressed an interest in meeting with the Pre-Law Club. I thanked Smith for her gift of $500 to the Annual Fund. She volunteered that she could never have gotten through college had it not been for her good professors and the scholarship support she received. We should consider her capacity to endow a scholarship focusing on English, pre-law or gender studies, given her stated interest in wanting to see more women in the legal profession. Next steps: Invite Smith to a campus lecture; consider nomination for alumni of the year or possible commencement speaker. Devise scholarship proposals for her consideration. Date for next contact: July 1, 2013.

The contact report will guide you and any other development officers or deans that come in contact with your alum. The information *per se* is useful, but it also helps avoid repetitive visits that cover the same ground, and guides future steps in Smith's cultivation. It is also a "hands off" message to other deans or development officers: they should not be approaching Smith for any reason without your prior knowledge. Once you have determined that your ask will be for a scholarship for the English department, you don't want another from an individual requesting support for a theatre production. A donor who has agreed to provide a major gift, and soon after is asked to support another project, will be confused and see disorder in the institution's fundraising operation.

No clear cut guidelines exist for when and for how much to make the ask. This is the art of fundraising; it all depends on perception, feel and a sense of readiness. This is why we describe the process in terms of a continuum. It can take six to eighteen months and anywhere from five to ten visits or encounters. Donors with an established giving history likely will expect to be approached about their next gift within a year of the expiration of their current pledge. Your visits to such individuals should have given you a good indication of what they are interested in supporting and to what extent. For others, the road is longer, built carefully step by step, moving from one spot on the giving continuum to the next.

> At one of our institutions, the dean and the major gift officer were reminded by one of our larger donors that his current pledge was about to end, and that he wanted to discuss his next gift. We set to work to determine when and how we would make our next ask. We examined his prior levels of support, the frequency with which he made donations, and how he had designated his gifts. In this instance, his primary areas of focus were Physics, his own undergraduate major, and Nursing, his wife's area of concentration. Over a period of several years he had endowed a number of scholarships, and set up research and faculty support funds in both program areas. We consulted with the departments in question about their ongoing needs and worked to match those with our donor's interests. We decided that we would ask this individual to become our first alumnus to give a seven-figure gift to the College, and identified a variety of funds his gift would support. In addition, we asked for funding to renovate an existing classroom where undergraduate physics would be taught in a new "active-learning" style, and provided a naming opportunity for the classroom. With our request near final form, we invited the donor to lunch specifically to discuss his next gift, and then carefully rehearsed our pitch to him. The lunch meeting went well, with the donor being particularly intrigued by the classroom renovation because, as he said, "he could see his money put to use more quickly." Through subsequent negotiation, discussion and modifications, we were successful in securing the College's first million-dollar plus gift from one of our alumni.

The million-dollar gift is unusual, but the same principles apply for those of a lesser amount: identify likely prospects, identify donor interest or passion, and estimate donor capacity. If you are working with a newer donor who is on the verge of her first major gift, it may be a bit more difficult to gauge what dollar amount to request, but you should be able to sense the donor's comfort level as a result of your conversations, and actual capacity based on research that can be undertaken by your University's Development Office. Conversation should also have identified areas of interest. If the donor has been quite specific and said she wanted to endow a scholarship supporting international travel, set up a meeting to provide details of what your minimum endowment levels are, draw up draft scholarship guidelines, as well as a draft gift agreement that you can present to the potential donor. Include at the meeting people in your organization who have detailed knowledge about the donor's area of interest. If the donor has been vague about areas of interest, you could present options based on your assessment of institutional needs, and invite the donor's response.

In examples just cited, significant preparation preceded the ask meeting. Now we should look at the meeting itself. Let's assume it occurred over lunch or morning or afternoon coffee. There will be some initial pleasantries, but it will be up to you to introduce the reason for the meeting fairly early on in the conversation. If you've gone about this the right way, all know why they are present. If you find it awkward to ask for money, as most of us do, to alleviate any jitters, practice what you will say. For example, "Miss Johnson, I want to thank you again for your interest in Noble University and in particular for students in our biology program. I'm thrilled that you are interested in endowing a scholarship. Today, I want to present draft guidelines for the Hilda Johnson Biology Scholarship." You should *not* be the first to speak after the ask. Wait for the donor to ask her questions, or respond to the proposal. Do your best to listen more than talk. If permissible, take notes. If the donor has any questions, be sure to answer them promptly. Continue to express gratitude for their interest and consideration. Before your meeting ends, be sure to have identified a point not too far into the future when you will be in contact about the donor's response to the proposal. Most donors, major or minor, are unlikely to commit immediately to a significant gift upon first receipt of a proposal. "I need to talk this over with my spouse," or "I'll have to consult with my financial advisor," are common and reasonable responses. Try to frame the questions you ask to elicit concrete answers. For example, "By what date do you think you will have come to a decision?" should generate a more specific response than, "How much longer do you need before you decide?"

Once the Gift has Been Given, or the Pledge Agreed to, how do you Continue to Work with the Donors to Ensure their Satisfaction?

The best way to thank people for their gifts is to remind them of the positive difference the gift has made from your stewardship. Building projects need to be undertaken when funding is forthcoming supporting them. Funds supporting students or faculty research or travel need to be allocated in accordance with donor intent. You are responsible for monitoring the expenditure of gifts and their benefits.

> At one of our institutions, the music department complained about a lack of scholarship funding supporting students. The dean examined the department's finances and realized, to his horror, that the department had fifteen to twenty endowed scholarships and over $100,000 in unspent income from those accounts. The department was not spending money that it had, or not spending it in sufficient amounts on an annual basis. The dean told the department that until it could demonstrate it was awarding the funding already available, he could not ask donors for further contributions. Over a multi-year period the carry-forward was substantially reduced.

This is an example of stewardship: the wise management, over time, of gifts.

Before donors provide follow-up gifts or foundations additional grants, they want to see evidence their dollars have brought effective change, and new programs have a "value-added" result. Persuasive evidence includes increased numbers of students brought into a program, increased graduation or retention rates, and other data traditionally accumulated by Institutional Research offices. But donors will be most moved when they see individual lives changed, faculty scholarship accomplished, programs or centers developed, equipment purchased, and facilities renovated and built. Whenever possible, make the evidence of their gifts personal, introducing them to scholarship recipients or current students and faculty who benefit from their generosity.

Conclusion

Given their myriad responsibilities, many deans are reluctant fundraisers. But as state and federal support dwindle, you must play a significant role in development. With commitment and proper strategies, your institution, however modest its present circumstances, can grow far more friends and supporters than would appear possible. Finding friends and raising funds is a long-term project. It should have been occurring prior to your arrival as dean. It is imperative for the fiscal health of your college that it continues after your departure. It will enrich your deanship, getting you out of the office and into compelling interactions with alumni, community supporters, and friends who support your institution, or are deeply grateful for the "leg up" education they received. Many of us may have approached fundraising with some trepidation but quickly grew to enjoy it because of the interactions it led to, and because it allowed a chance to "tell the good stories" of the college. It is too easy to get caught up in the administrative weeds and so lose sight of the transformative power of higher education. At the end of the day, we are not asking for money for ourselves, but for our institutions, our faculty and staff, and above all, for our students.

Arts and Sciences organizationally into three colleges, including the College of Humanities and Social and Behavioral Sciences. CHSBS (for which Pamela Gates serves as dean) is the largest college on campus with eight departments and ten interdisciplinary programs, yet its name has been a challenge for anyone outside of the academy. As noted previously in this book, most alumni associate themselves with their degree, department, or major program but may not feel any particular connection to the college or school from which they graduated. Given that to some degree every department or program within the College is engaged in either public service or global citizenship, a new administrative arm (The School of Public Service and Global Citizenship) was created to market what they do in a focused way and provide opportunities for donors to support that work.

At the *University of Nebraska at Omaha* (UNO), the idea that the College of Arts and Sciences (for which David Boocker serves as dean) is a liberal arts college within a metropolitan university is stated in the college's mission statement and, indeed the college is acknowledged as the major proponent for the liberal arts. Just outside the dean's office is a donor recognition board that thanks donors for their "support of academic excellence in the Liberal Arts." The College of Arts and Sciences, the oldest and largest of the six colleges at the University, is comprised of 14 departments and six interdisciplinary programs. The University as a whole currently is focused on three core values: academic excellence, student focus, and community engagement, and like CMU, UNO's commitment to community is critically important. For example, UNO is a regional leader in service learning opportunities for students, with 2,300 students in 121 service-related courses. Similarly, many of the college's fundraising priorities and outcomes are connected to this focus on engagement.

From these two examples alone, we can recognize that what constitutes Arts and Sciences varies dramatically from campus to campus, which complicates the ability for anyone to create a unified strategy for making the case for Arts and Sciences. But the values espoused by a liberal arts education need not be determined by an institution's organizational structure; instead we need to recognize that a complete education, in which all fields of human knowledge contained within the humanities, social sciences, and sciences, is the product of a liberal arts education. This point becomes even more important in today's higher education climate in which the vocational emphasis of getting a degree unfortunately is trumping the greater purpose of pursuing an education for its own sake—a change that many Arts and Sciences alums and donors lament. As a result, many proponents of the liberal arts are finding that the liberal arts has become a hard sell today because the traditional liberal arts education is not seen by students and/or their parents as preparing students for a specific vocation. To counter this concern, proponents of the liberal arts can no longer isolate themselves from these vocational concerns. As he writes in *Why Choose the Liberal Arts*, Mark William Roche finds it "not only ironic but also appealing that the very education we elevate for its intrinsic value cultivates virtues that serve meaningful external ends and prepares students for the needs and challenges of practical life" (University of Notre Dean Press, 2010, p 51).

While the history of the role and scope of the liberal arts falls outside the primary purpose of this essay, as deans of Arts and Sciences we have to remain constantly vigilant that our colleges have strong messages promoting the values of the liberal arts. Nor is the need for a defense about the role and values of the liberal arts a new problem. In 1964, The Association of American Colleges published *Reflections on the Role of Liberal Education* (a reprint of Volume L, Number 2 of *Liberal Education*), a collection designed "to initiate debate on the role of liberal education in a democratic society in the latter part of the twentieth century, and more particularly, the place of the liberal arts college in American education." Most interesting in this description is the focus on the liberal arts college. In 2014, only a quarter of CCAS member institutions are traditional liberal arts colleges, and for this reason, making the case for Arts and Sciences and the liberal arts becomes even more critical for those of us who work in institutions where Arts and Sciences programs are perceived by some students as failing to address the immediacy of occupational goals.

There is an abundance of literature written in defense of the liberal arts promoting the idea that strengthening a university's liberal education component has less to do with preparing graduates for an entry level job than in producing educated citizens for a democratic society. *Liberal Education*, a publication of the Association of American Colleges and Universities (AAC&U), remains an essential source for current trends in higher education. The Liberal Education and America's Promise (LEAP) initiative championed by AAC&U *(http://www.aacu.org/leap/)* provides the best framework for discussing the goals and values of a twenty-first century liberal education. LEAP focuses on "the kinds of learning that Americans need to thrive in a knowledge intensive economy, a globally engaged democracy, and society where innovation is the key to progress and success." AAC&U's recent report, *How Liberal Arts and Sciences Majors Fare in Employment* (Debra Humphreys and Patrick Kelly, 2014), "provides a much-needed corrective to claims that most liberal arts— those with a degree in a humanities, arts, or social science field—are unemployed and unemployed … [and] tracks the success rates of liberal arts majors and documents how society benefits from liberal arts graduates." The work of AAC&U is invaluable because it helps us understand what an educated citizen is expected to learn in the 21st century, how to explain the value-added derived from a college education and, perhaps most important, it helps us understand the right relationship between undergraduate education and preparation for and long-term success in employment.

Another important resource is The Council of Independent Colleges, which has a website devoted to promoting the liberal arts *(http://www.cic.edu/Research-and-Data/Liberal-Arts/Campaign/Pages/Promote-the-Liberal-Arts.aspx)*. Here you can find resources such as op-eds from university presidents, important research and data, along with specific recommendations about how to promote the liberal arts, such as: writing an op-ed article promoting the values of your college for your local newspaper; speaking to a local Rotary Club about the mission and values of your college; using your college magazine or newsletter or Facebook page to share stories about how the liberal arts shaped your career and the careers of your alumni. And to these we want to suggest that you always engage your alumni, who can be your best spokespersons for the value of a liberal arts education. Encourage your departments and programs to invite alumni back to campus to meet with students and faculty. Invite your alumni to speak to students about the value of the liberal arts education they received and how it helps them to achieve success. Explain to students who come to you for funding that generous alumni gave the dollars you have available to help them. And keep the members of your college informed about the ongoing debate about liberal arts by forwarding stories from the *Chronicle of Higher Education*, Inside Higher Ed, *University Business*, *Liberal Education*, and other sources. These strategies, while not necessarily directly related to successful fundraising, are useful in creating a vision for the college that can guide your development philosophy and priorities.

Setting the Stage for Fundraising: Build a Vision Using Priorities

While most colleges of Arts and Sciences have highly refined messages directed at students about the power of a liberal arts education, for our purposes here we have to consider how to translate these messages to prospective donors. As dean, your goal is to raise funds to support priorities within your college—priorities that in the development phase often require conversations with prospective donors about the general state of higher education and how your college is serving the needs and interests of students.

> *(DB)* As a new dean at UNO some years ago, my first meeting with prospective donors focused on how I was planning to brand the College of Arts and Sciences. More recently I met with donor who was interested in how the college was trying to maintain a connection with its historical past; in the end, we agreed on a regular feature in our college magazine featuring recollections by a retired faculty member or former student.

> *(PSG)* Given that I have been at Central Michigan for nearly three decades, alumni often ask me if I remember certain faculty members, and sometimes I do, which adds an immediate level of compatibility. These discussions often turn to the role of liberal arts. Our experience is that alumni are

often concerned about the state of the liberal arts in higher education, and as dean your role is to assure them that you are a strong proponent of the liberal arts.

The point is that successful fundraising is built on these kinds of conversations, on which meaningful relationships are built. As dean, one of the most important things you can do is meet with alumni, listen to their stories, memories, and connect them with insights in the programs and faculty who are now teaching this generation of students. The result is a shared sense of the history of the institution and a shared personal experience of the importance of the institution to you and to them. It is important that as dean your presentation focuses generally on the fundamental role of the college of Arts and Sciences, and on making a case for a good fit between the donor of your college's programmatic needs and priorities. This last point is critically important because, more than anything else, donors want to know that their contributions will make a difference to students, faculty, and/or the larger community.

As dean, you are responsible for establishing priorities for your college of Arts and Sciences. Work with your departments and programs to identify the best development opportunities. This process can be challenging. In Chapter 3 Danilowicz and Hayes discuss how "Arts and Sciences is a complex college, and you will have alumni-rich and alumni-poor departments, both in numbers and in gift potential." Although they recommend engaging all units, this may prove difficult with limited development support personnel, and the lack of attention some departments and programs will give to development. Development strategies for Arts and Sciences are subject to the same realities and prospects that drive programmatic decisions about all college priorities.

Within the broader contexts of each University, establishing overarching priorities for a college of Arts and Sciences can be challenging because our colleges are large and intellectually diverse. There is no simple way to establish priorities but there must be some sense of fairness in their selection. One possibility is to prioritize by using disciplinary clusters: humanities, social sciences, natural and physical sciences/math, cultural studies. Within each of these you can designate at least one department/program for development based on four major factors:

1. *Identify programs of excellence in your college.* It is easier to promote programs to donors in which students and faculty have a track record by whatever measures you use to gauge success.

2. *Identify programs where there is a faculty champion* who will work effectively with the college development officer to spearhead the development opportunity. The most successful departments/programs in acquiring funds are those that share in building a vision for the college of Arts and Sciences and who engage the college process.

3. *Choose college priorities that align with the University's priorities.* Your priorities must align with those of your University for several reasons. First, donors like to know that their gifts will support the greatest good. Second, because major fundraising involves teamwork, it is absolutely necessary that your president know your development priorities that support campus priorities, since they interact frequently with major donors.

> At UNO, the College of Arts and Sciences has been able to achieve some of our College priorities because we have made the Chancellor (Nebraska's term) able to make our case for us with donors. Two years ago, the Deans' Forum met with the Senior Vice-Chancellor to establish major academic priorities, which were then turned into University of Nebraska Foundation development priorities, designated as 1) STEM Education, 2) Sustainability, 3) Global Engagement, and 4) Early Childhood Education. These cross-campus priorities were ideal for Arts and Sciences, because they were interdisciplinary and included an engagement component. The College of Arts and Sciences had

a vested interest in all four priorities—which could not be said for any of the other five Colleges. Subsequently, the NU Foundation convened a meeting of major donors to announce these priorities and asked for community volunteers to participate in a strategic planning process with engaged faculty for each. That has ultimately led to successful fundraising with the help of the community volunteers.

Central Michigan University recently approved a new strategic plan that emphasizes several priorities—one of which includes the role of public service and global citizenship for our students. Consequently, the College of Humanities and Social and Behavioral Sciences has engaged faculty, students, alumni, and donors to become champions for the funding of internships, study abroad opportunities, and recruitment of international students. Faculty often contact the development officer to alert us to where they are traveling for conferences or research opportunities so we can arrange for them to meet with alumni in the area, take them to dinner, or host a reception if the numbers merit a larger venue. Depending upon the engagement level of the alumni/donor prospect, the development officer may make the trip as well.

4. *Choose college priorities that have a component that links its successful completion to community engagement and student success.* Many donors want their gifts to have a tangible and visible impact on their local community and/or on creating enhanced opportunities for students, such as study abroad discipline-specific scholarships that reward student excellence.

Your development officer is critically important in helping to build your fundraising plan and must be viewed as a member of your college strategic planning team. To be a successful development officer for Arts and Sciences, a development officer needs to understand the complicated structure and relationships that make up your college. You should meet regularly; at UNO and CMU, the dean and development officer meet an hour or more once a week and talk on the phone frequently. The development officers update their deans on the current status of open requests and discuss the programmatic developments in the college, which frequently turns into ideas for fundraising. Without this kind of teamwork, your development officer cannot work to identify prospective donors for your priorities. Once you agree on a priority, your development officer will then work as needed with her/his development colleagues as well as the appropriate department, program, and/or faculty member(s) to gather the knowledge needed to proceed with planning and engagement with donors.

Focused Planning on Your Priorities

Having established fundraising priorities for your college, you now have to develop strategies for moving forward with fundraising. In many ways, this is the most important and difficult step in the fundraising process because you have to decide what to raise money for within the context of the priorities and needs of your college. It's one thing to say that you will raise money for political science, and it's another thing to say you are looking for people to donate specifically for professorships, faculty and/or student research, a lecture series, and teaching awards. The best fundraising opportunities are created when specific goals are developed within the context of department and college priorities. Making the case for Arts and Sciences is about making a case for a good fit between the donor and your college's programmatic needs—be it scholarships, endowed-speaker series, endowed professorships, and even endowed chairs. You might ask yourself and your team: what are we trying to achieve with this speaker series focused on politics and public policy at Central Michigan University? What are we trying to accomplish when we ask donors to support the STEM Education priority at the University of Nebraska at Omaha?

The following cases provide examples of effective planning that led to successful fundraising initiatives. Such planning begins with an idea, in these cases first suggested by donors who wanted to partner with the college and University in reaching a common goal.

> *(PSG)* At CMU we were approached by a donor with the idea to create an endowed speaker series designed to emphasize integrity in politics and public service by working to supplant negativity and partisanship with creativity and innovation in shaping future public policy. The series would seek out guest speakers whose work embodies the ideals set forth by Michigan leaders like Philip A. Hart, U.S. senator (1958–1976) and William G. Milliken, governor (1969–1982), providing a forum where students may listen, learn and engage in meaningful dialogue focusing on a range of current and past political and policy-making issues.

> *(DB)* The STEM Education initiative at UNO began with the impetus of a donor who wanted to increase the pipeline of students moving into teacher education in mathematics. We were asked to develop strategies to identify more and better students interested in pursuing mathematics education. This quickly expanded into a discussion about how to recruit and retain more students in all STEM majors. Soon after, STEM Education/Learning was designated a UNO campus priority. Collaboration among administrators and faculty from different disciplines and colleges facilitated this discussion at UNO. In the end, it was determined that it would be critically important to recruit and retain star STEM science and math faculty who would take the lead in formalizing the network between K-12 and UNO in the areas of science and math. We worked with STEM faculty leaders and the NU Foundation to develop a strategic plan to seek funds for this initiative.

Promoting the Vision to Donors

Once you have a good idea to present to donors, you will need to work with your entire team to strategize to identify prospective donors and how to approach them. As noted by Danilowicz and Hayes in Chapter 3, "You are the chief academic officer for the college, which means your development officer will rely on you [and participating faculty] to be able to communicate (in lay terms) the academic vision of the college and its potential programs to potential donors." And in Chapter 4, Trela, Finkelstein and Vermeulen list six appropriate "steps to finding friends and raising money." Your development officer is critical to this process, since he/she will usually have a list of prospective donors that may have an interest in your project. In other cases, your officer will create a list of prospective donors through research or by consulting friends of the college. Your development officer may also make initial contact with prospective donors. Selling your college's vision to donors is grounded on two main strategies: planning and relationship building.

Referring to the ideas that had been proposed by alumni, described above,

> *(PSG)* The endowed speaker's series at CMU and its initial $500,000 endowment came together within a six-month period. After the donor came to us with the idea for such a series—and we clarified what we could accomplish through such a series—my development officer and I met with both politicians' families to seek their approval and support. Once we had their permission to move forward, the campaign accelerated and we were able to identify major donors who, while not all alumni of our University, believed in the value and purpose of the project. (We were also fortunate to be able to take advantage of a University match on the payout if we were able to reach the projected goal by the end of the year—which we did.) It was intensive work, but one that has paid off for our students, faculty, and community by having the ability to bring key political figures to campus to speak.

> *(DB)* The STEM priority at UNO was initiated by a donor who established two $1-million Community Chairs—one in the College of Education and one in the Department of

environmental or other research focused on the public good.

CMU's College of Humanities and Social and Behavioral Sciences has enjoyed similar successes, having raised $6 million in the past five years with at least another $1.5 million gift projected for 2014. Some of the recent successes are seen in the following:

- The Great Lakes Institute of Sustainable Systems, to promote academic programs, research, community outreach, and campus operations dedicated to the advancement of sustainable systems.
- The Endowed Lecture in the Study of Dictatorship, Democracy and Genocide, which brings to CMU distinguished scholars to discuss the past, present, and future of worldwide genocide, Holocaust and mass murders in Africa, Southeast Asia, and Central America.
- The Olga J. and G. Roland Denison Visiting Professorship of Native American Studies, to support an endowed scholar that enhances the capability of the NAS program at CMU and to help build the relationship between the Saginaw Chippewa Indian Tribe, CMU, and the Mount Pleasant Community.
- The Field Leadership Reaction Course, designed for ROTC cadets to prepare for the leadership training they experience between their junior and senior year of college at Joint Base Lewis-McChord in Washington State. The course will also benefit other University and community members who wish to use the course for team building initiatives.

The CMU and UNO stories illustrate strategies for establishing priorities discussed in "Setting the Stage for Fundraising." Almost every example contains a goal to serve the community, either in terms of engaging the community in important political or social issues or in terms of working with area schools to improve teacher education. Making the case for colleges of Arts and Sciences and identifying projects worthy of private funding demands a vision that excites prospective donors. They understand and appreciate that their major gifts will support the public role the college must have to remain viable in today's society. In many cases, successful fundraising efforts extend beyond alumni to include members of our community or state who believe in the purpose of our campaign.

So far, our examples focus on strategies for acquiring major gifts for Arts and Sciences. But as a dean of Arts and Sciences, you must recognize the value of all gifts, large and small. If you are asked to support a general mailing, recognize that while the yield may be relatively small, an accumulation of small gifts in a general college excellence fund allows you some flexibility to support important activities to enrich student education. The letter itself should explain to donors who might be inclined to give that their gifts matter. Provide examples of how their gift allowed you to send student Jason to a professional conference in Pittsburgh or Megan to the Newberry in Chicago to complete research on her thesis. Take note of gifts larger than expected and any accompanying correspondence from the donor. Your development officer can sometimes use donor responses as follow-up leads for more and greater gifts.

> *(DB)* At UNO, I have used the letter to promote the values of undergraduate research, which is a major initiative in our college and University. While students have access to some funding in our Office of Research and Creative Activity thanks to a student fee, they rely on departments and the college for travel support. In response to one mailing focused on undergraduate research, one donor stepped up to establish a new fund to support that priority.

> *(PSG)* At CMU, we include a donor solicitation insert with every college newsletter that is sent out via regular mail or email. This provides alumni and donors an opportunity to support a program that has been featured within the newsletter, since it is often the student success stories that attract their interest. As a result of a particularly strong program where students are required to study abroad, one donor has provided a gift to support future students who wish to participate.

Resources
Appendix A

Workshops, Conferences, Training

SPONSOR: Council of Colleges of Arts & Sciences (CCAS)
www.ccas.net
SAMPLE OFFERINGS:
- Deans & Development
- Making the Case for Supporting the Liberal Arts

SPONSOR: Association of Fundraising Professionals
www.afpnet.org
SAMPLE OFFERINGS:
- The Fundraising Leadership Boot Camp: Evolving from Good to Great
- Millennial Motivation: What Makes Millennial Want To Give

SPONSOR: Council for the Advancement and Support of Education (CASE)
www.case.org
SAMPLE OFFERINGS:
- Development for Deans and Academic Leaders
- Advanced Development for Deans and Academic Leaders

SPONSOR: Academic Resources
www.advancementresources.org
SAMPLE OFFERINGS:
- Professional Fundraising Workshop for Deans, Department Chairs, and Aspiring Academic Leaders
- Philanthropic Practices for Deans and Other Academic Leaders
- Development Skills for Deans and Other Academic Leaders
- Professional Fundraising Workshop for Deans, Department Chairs, and Aspiring Academic Leaders

SPONSOR: Academic Impressions
www.academicimpressions.com
SAMPLE OFFERINGS:

- Smarter Thinking for Annual Giving
- Building Fundraising Partnerships between Deans and Development Officers

SPONSOR: Lilly Family School of Philanthropy – Women's Philanthropy Institute
www.philanthropy.iupui.edu/womens-philanthropy-institute
SAMPLE OFFERINGS:

- Developing Major Gifts
- Interpersonal Communication for Fundraising

Publications

Buchanan, Peter McE. (ed.) *Handbook of Institutional Advancement* (3rd edition). CASE, 2000.

Council for the Advancement and Support of Education. *Fearless Fund Raising: A Guide for Faculty and Deans.* Reprinted from Currents, the CASE member magazine, 2000.

Hunt, P. *Development for Academic Leaders: A Practical Guide for Fundraising Success.* San Francisco: Jossey-Bass, 2012.

Hodson, J.B. and Speck, B.W. (ed). *Perspectives on Fund Raising: New Directions for Higher Education, Number 149.* San Francisco: Jossey-Bass, 2010.

Hilenski, F.A. (ed.) *Unit Development Officer's Handbook, The.* Washington, D.C.: CASE, 2002.

Worth, Michael. *Leading the Campaign: Advancing Colleges and Universities.* Rowan and Littlefield, 2010.

Index